Innovation in Social Welfare and Human Services

Innovation is an oft-heard buzzword in both public and private sectors concerned with the organization and delivery of services to vulnerable individuals. This thoughtful volume explores what innovation might actually involve in the context of contemporary human services.

Highlighting both the importance and utility of innovation but also promoting a more reflective approach, the book distinguishes between innovation and improvement and discusses the relevant differences between private sector, public sector and non-profit organizations. It looks at how innovation is often as much a result of the power relations between the involved actors, and the structural context, as a result of popularly identified "drivers" and "barriers". Including numerous case studies, the book illustrates and explains innovations in welfare services at different levels, looking at the macro level (innovations in social policy), the meso level (innovations at the organizational level) and the micro level (user-driven innovations).

Arguing that innovation is nothing new in human services, the authors emphasize the importance of innovation being developed and supported by those working within those organizations. New and creative solutions to problems encountered in everyday work by front-line workers can be taken up to improve services provided and make a difference for service users, rather than change being externally imposed upon them by those without insider knowledge.

Innovation in Social Welfare and Human Services is an important read for researchers and practitioners interested in the administration, leadership and organization of social services.

Rolf Rønning is a Professor of Social Policy at Lillehammer University College, Norway. He has, for many years, conducted research and been published in the field of welfare policy. His main research interests now lie in the area of innovation in the public sector, with welfare services as the main focus. His recent publications include *Framing Innovation in Public Service Sectors*.

Marcus Knutagård is a Researcher and Senior Lecturer in the School of Social Work at Lund University, Sweden. His current research interests include work on the moral geography of homelessness, category formation in the field of homelessness, and social policy and housing. With colleagues at Lund University and Lillehammer University College, he has recently written a book on innovations in welfare services with a special focus on social innovations.

Routledge Advances in Health and Social Policy

New titles

Health Care Reform and Globalisation
The US, China and Europe in Comparative Perspective
Edited by Peggy Watson

Power and Welfare
Understanding Citizens' Encounters with State Welfare
Nanna Mik-Meyer and Kaspar Villadsen

International Perspectives on Elder Abuse
Amanda Phelan

Mental health Services for Vulnerable Children and Young People
Supporting children who are, or have been, in foster care
Michael Tarren-Sweeney and Arlene Vetere

Providing Compassionate Health Care
Challenges in Policy and Practice
Edited by Sue Shea, Robin Wynyard and Christos Lionis

Teen Pregnancy and Parenting
Rethinking the Myths and Misperceptions
Keri Weed, Jody S. Nicholson and Jaelyn R. Farris

The Invisible Work of Nurses
Hospitals, Organisation and Healthcare
Davina Allen

Domestic Violence in Diverse Contexts
A Re-examination of Gender
Sarah Wendt and Lana Zannettino

Innovation in Social Welfare and Human Services
Rolf Rønning and Marcus Knutagård

Forthcoming titles

M-health in Developing Countries
Design and Implementation Perspectives on Using Mobiles in Healthcare
Arul Chib

Alcohol Policy in Europe
Delivering the WHO Ideal?
Shane Butler, Karen Elmeland, Betsy Thom and James Nicholls

International Perspectives on Support for Trafficked Women
Developing a Model for Service Provision
Delia Rambaldini-Gooding

Maternity Services and Policy in an International Context
Risk, Citizenship and Welfare Regimes
Edited by Patricia Kennedy and Naonori Kodate

Social Development and Social Work Perspectives on Social Protection
Edited by Julie Drolet

Innovation in Social Welfare and Human Services

Rolf Rønning and Marcus Knutagård

LONDON AND NEW YORK

First published 2015 by Routledge

2 Park Square, Milton Park, Abingdon, Oxfordshire OX14 4RN
52 Vanderbilt Avenue, New York, NY 10017

Routledge is an imprint of the Taylor & Francis Group, an informa business

First issued in paperback 2019

British Library Cataloguing-in-Publication Data
A catalogue record for this book is available from the British Library

Library of Congress Cataloging in Publication Data
A catalog record for this book has been requested

ISBN: 978-0-415-73126-3 (hbk)
ISBN: 978-0-367-34578-5 (pbk)

Typeset in Times New Roman
by Wearset Ltd, Boldon, Tyne and Wear

Contents

Preface

We participated in the Joint World Conference on Social Work and Social Development in Stockholm in 2012, where we presented perspectives from our Swedish book about innovation in social welfare services. Innovation was not a topic discussed elsewhere at the conference, but we found that the topic got some attention. When we were asked by Grace McInnes of Routledge to write an English book on the subject, we saw this as an opportunity to elaborate on our own thinking and to reach a larger audience.

We were four authors in the Swedish version, and only two of us have continued the work on innovation in welfare services. However, without the common work in the first book, and the support we got then, it would not have been possible to write the present version. Thanks to our generous colleagues, Cecilia Heule and Hans Swärd, and also to the Swedish editor, Peter Söderholm, for their support then, and for giving us the rights to use what we wanted in a new version.

This is not a translation of an existing book. We have both developed our thinking over the last two years and we wanted to write an international book. Two of the chapters are completely new, and most of the others are totally rewritten. It is actually a new book.

Both authors are responsible for the whole book, but Marcus has had the main responsibility for Chapters 1, 3 and 6, and Rolf for the rest.

Rolf Rønning and Marcus Knutagård
Lillehammer and Lund, July 2014

1 Introduction

If we are to better the future, we must disturb the present.

(Catherine Booth)[1]

Introduction

Like Catherine Booth, most people are, and have been, engaged in improving the quality of life for themselves or other people. This book is written for students, practitioners and researchers in social welfare and human services, many of whom are concerned with improving the quality of life for vulnerable groups. This book may hopefully give some new perspectives and inspiration for this work.

Both service users and employees within social welfare and human services are facing the demand for more efficiency, and the consequences of efforts to realize it. Employees can feel inadequate even when they stretch the rubber band too far. Into this context, innovation is introduced as an imperative to be even more efficient – one more demand. It is not surprising, then, that people in this sector seem to be rather reluctant to join the innovation bandwagon. That is, at least, our impression from our communication with people in the field. We know that staff are continuously concerned with improving services, but it may be a big step to use knowledge and tools from innovative work systematically in their own efforts. The sector needs new and creative solutions, and it is important that these solutions take into account the special demands in the sector, both the tacit and the codified knowledge of service users and employees. They should be the innovators, rather than being "innovated" by others. If not, we risk throwing the baby out with the bathwater. We hope that this book can both save the baby and inspire new and creative ways of thinking in the field.

Innovation has become a buzzword, and seems to be positively loaded in the public debate. Many experts are eager to impose on us their version of what innovation is. Welfare services are very visible aspects of public expenditure and are important for us all. We still have unmet expectations of the services, despite an increase in the budgets. Doing things better is of course possible in these services, and people in the field should be the main contributors in realizing this.

This book is meant to give a framework for such an engagement.

When we think of innovations, we still most often envision types of tangible object made of plastic or metal – maybe technological gadgets or inventions (Nelson 2011). However, innovations can also be non-tangible, such as new ways of organizing a service. We argue in this book that the welfare state can be seen as an innovation. The welfare sector might not be the first thing that comes to mind when we think of innovation. During the industrial era, the focus was on technological innovations, but the emergence of service-based societies has created an increased need for innovations that are social in nature. Critical junctures, especially during a time of crisis, can bring about systemic change. During these transformative periods, the possibility for new innovations to take shape grows. Understanding a crisis – realizing that we cannot continue doing what we have done before – can give fertile ground for systemic change.

"Welfare" means that people should fare well through life's various stages (Daly 2011). Welfare also has to do with people's living conditions in terms of opportunities for a reasonable livelihood, whether they have an attachment to the labour market or not. Welfare includes health, housing, working conditions and basic social security.

Social networks, private companies, social enterprises and NGOs can all be producers of welfare services, but if a society wants to create rights and basic social security for larger groups, public commitments are required. When these commitments are met, one can speak of a welfare state.

The term "welfare state" came into general use after the Second World War as a designation of democratic countries with market economies and comprehensive social policies (Olofsson 2009). Sometimes the term "welfare democracies", or "welfare societies", is used for countries with well-developed welfare services.

Since the same welfare services can be delivered by many different actors, Esping-Andersen (1990) introduced the term "welfare regime" in a comparison of the European welfare societies, to describe differences in delivery models. The public sector (the state and municipalities), market actors and civil society can all be service providers. Civil society, or the third sector, includes here non-profit actors, neighbourhood services and family care.

Different countries have developed distinctively different combinations. The Scandinavian or "social democratic" model gives much of the responsibility for establishing, financing and providing the services to public authorities. The "liberal model" (the US, the UK) leaves more to the market, while the "continental model" puts the responsibility for many deliveries onto the third sector, and also through participation in the labour market. All of the regimes can be said to be welfare societies, but the environments for innovation are different. New combinations of service providers are created today, both hybrid organizations and social entrepreneurs. These new constructions have their own balancing acts. They have to handle different institutional logics that are not congruent (Gidron and Hasenfeld 2012). They will be discussed further in Chapters 3 and 4.

Social policy is an important instrument in welfare societies to prevent and solve social problems and create social security. One of the tasks of social policy is to provide various benefits to people in cases of work injury, unemployment, old age, parenthood and illness. Another task is to produce or administer various welfare services within health care and social services. There is a clear connection between social citizenship and the welfare society, and the membership rights are most comprehensive in the Nordic model (Nygård 2013; Johansson 2008).

The need for innovation in the welfare sector has differed during different time periods. During the rise of the welfare state (1880–1940), several large-scale reforms took place in Europe. The period after the Second World War (1945–1980) is usually seen as a period during which we had a "strong society" with high employment and high economic growth, generating high incomes for the public sector. This provided opportunities for further expansion and refinement of the welfare state, such as the expansion of day-care centres and schools, and of higher education. The period was also marked by a significant optimism.

The emergence and consolidation of the welfare state have been characterized by ambiguity, ambivalence and struggle. The type of large-scale reforms, of which the rise of the welfare state is an example, can in today's language be called innovations – and several welfare state reforms may be seen as radical innovations (see Chapter 2).

Women entering the labour market during the 1970s and 1980s created a radical change. This contributed to a great need for childcare and parental leave. Several convergent factors and changes created a demand for new solutions to deal with newly arising social challenges. One solution was to build a functioning parental insurance system. Since the scope and speed of women's participation in the labour force varied between European countries, the public engagement in offering these services varied. While social security for (male) workers had been dominant in welfare states before the Second World War, women's entrance into the labour market created a need for care services (Anttonen 1997), both for the elderly and for children. In Nordic countries, the public sector took the main responsibility here, and they now have a very high female participation in the workforce. In countries with different welfare regimes, the public sector was also engaged in this work, but the provision of the services was shared with other actors.

Since 1980, there has been a re-examination of the "strong society", and the public responsibility for welfare services has been questioned. The growing cost of the public part of the pension system has triggered a remodelling of the system in many countries, and the burden of the growth is now to a larger extent carried by pensioners themselves. The main challenge has been to make the system both economically and socially sustainable. Low birth rates in Europe and an increasingly ageing population have raised questions whether we will have enough carers to care in the future, and also worries for the costs. Many countries in the Western world today are trying to develop a cheaper and more efficient welfare system. The restructuring of the welfare state and welfare services is evident. Parts of the welfare state have been questioned.

One solution can be to decrease the scope of services offered and let people take more of the responsibility themselves. In many cases, such withdrawals will have a social bias and hit hardest those with the least resources. Changes are always a choice between values.

Welfare deliveries have also begun to take other forms, such as the privatization of services previously provided by the state, an enhanced role for third sector organizations, and increased competition. In this context, the call for innovations and innovative strategies has increased.

The sharing of duties between public and private actors has often been a source of conflict between left- and right-wing politicians, where those on the left wing have wanted more public responsibility than their counterparts on the right. Since the late 1970s, neo-liberal and right-wing politicians have gained political power in many European countries, and these neo-liberal winds have also contributed to move the position of the left. The neo-liberal model for reorganizing the public sector, New Public Management (NPM), therefore also received support from "modernized" social democrats (such as Tony Blair in the UK). This change of the political landscape has definitely triggered the search for innovations within welfare services. NPM will be discussed at greater length in the following chapters.

When the business sector can point to studies that conclude that 50–80 per cent of economic growth depends on innovation and new knowledge (Helpman 2004), then it is not surprising that innovation receives much attention. If we use this estimate as the model for the "improvement" (and savings) innovation can bring about in the public sector, the pressure to innovate will be significant.

There are several reasons to be interested in, and to believe in, the effect of innovations on social welfare and human services in particular. Examples of cost reductions in private business are mentioned. Technological developments and innovations promise both to improve welfare and human services and to make them less costly. The expectation of innovation in welfare and human services is high on the political agenda and many put their trust in innovation as a solution to the problems that we are facing in a globalized world – in both developing and developed countries. In developing countries, innovation is considered essential to promoting social development. In developed countries, innovation is the solution to sustaining social welfare and human services without increasing the tax burden. The EU wants, through its Europe 2020 strategy, to create smart, sustainable and inclusive growth for all, even the poor. The EU stresses the importance of finding new and innovative solutions, especially in the social economy. However, so far no really revolutionary and radical solutions have been launched.

Public organizations, and particularly welfare services such as care and social welfare, are often seen as cumbersome, sluggish and not so innovative, in contrast to the dynamic and innovative business community. However, some studies show that there is more innovation in the public sector than in the private sector (Earl 2002; Earl 2004; Koch *et al.* 2005). The public sector is, and has been, an active driver of innovations:

most of the radical, revolutionary innovations that have fuelled the dynamics of capitalism – from railroads to the Internet, to modern-day nanotechnology and pharmaceuticals – trace the most courageous, early and capital-intensive "entrepreneurial" investments back to the State.

(Mazzucato 2013, p. 3)

In this book, we want to direct the gaze towards innovations that are emerging in the public sector in order to address social problems. Market actors and voluntary organizations can carry out the welfare services that are created, but the responsibility for the provision and funding of welfare services still falls on the public sector. Welfare is a very broad concept and covers a range of areas. Our examples of innovations are collected primarily from the public sector.

A few words about the terms. The focus of this book is on social welfare and human services. These terms are used in different ways, and to cover different services in different countries. In textbooks in the UK, for instance, it has been common to include education and housing in discussions about social policy. In Nordic countries, education is a separate field. The term "human services" might be more recognized in the US. Human services are services that are directed towards people. In some ways, human services can be seen as including not only welfare and health services, but also social work. Sometimes a distinction is drawn between human services and social work, where the latter is seen as being conducted by professionals who are "street-level bureaucrats" working directly with their clients (Lipsky 1980). Human services tend to be described as having a more managerial focus. The term has also been used for a movement, based in human psychology, that wanted to put more attention on the whole person than specialized disciplines within welfare services were supposed to do. In our book, we use the terms to cover the services dedicated to helping people to have a "normal" and decent life. Many professionals contribute here, from medical doctors, psychologists, social workers and nurses, to occupational therapists, speech therapists and others. We hope our book is relevant for everyone who spends parts of their life in increasing the quality of life for other people. The challenges for the services are also challenges for all of the contributors.

In Chapter 2, we define the term "innovation" and take a closer look at how it is used and its origin. We also discuss some of the common taxonomies in the literature on innovation.

In Chapter 3, we focus on social innovation, and especially on the social innovation process.

In Chapter 4, we discuss the particular significance that innovation has within the public sector and how the concept can be understood within this realm. When innovations are taken into the public sphere, they become part of the political struggle in society, and different groups aim to realize their interests through innovations. Political power is important for realizing, and understanding, how innovations are decided and implemented. This is discussed in further detail in Chapter 5.

In Chapter 6, we highlight social innovations with the help of examples of innovations at different levels. We distinguish between innovations at a macro, meso and micro level. The different examples of innovations are intended to shed light on how innovations at one level also affect other levels. We will highlight user-driven innovation and how service users themselves can be a driving force in the social innovation process.

In Chapter 7, we discuss common obstacles and challenges to innovation, in addition to those mentioned in the previous chapters. In spite of the fact that many people want to innovate, it is not easy either to get support for or to implement creative ideas in practice.

In the final chapter, we describe and discuss some strategies that can be used to innovate within welfare services. Many roads are accessible if we want to start the journey towards establishing a culture of innovation.

A purpose of this book is to demystify the concept of innovation, while also drawing attention to the innovative work that goes on in the welfare sector. It can be difficult to observe innovation practices since they are often gradual and slow processes. Changes within welfare services seem to be incremental rather than radical transformations. Institutions within human services have a tendency to fall for fads and other trends, of which only a few will be sustainable innovations (Best 2006). It is interesting to see that a method that has been abandoned in one context can find a new application within another organizational field. Brunsson (2006) points out that organizations often try to reform the work they do so that they will be more rational. However, reorganizations rarely lead to fulfilling this goal. Hopefully this book will encourage readers to develop a critical and reflective approach to innovations in their own sector. At the same time, we hope that readers will be creative and use their own expertise to innovate.

In this book, we use the term "innovation" for much of the change and development work that has been going on in social welfare and human services. We do this because "innovation" has become the accepted term, and because the concept of innovation, in the way the term is used today, involves a broad variety of activities.

Note

1 Catherine Booth (1829–1890) established, together with her husband William, the Salvation Army. The quote can be found on http://christian-quotes.ochristian.com/Catherine-Booth-Quotes/.

2   What is innovation?

When you discover you are riding a dead horse, the best strategy is to dismount.
(Tribal wisdom of the Dakota Indians)

In this chapter, we will explain the meaning of innovation and introduce some important properties that are useful in discussing innovation as an activity. Innovations must be understood in the context of time and space. In modern economies, there is a move away from focusing on production (of goods) towards focusing on services. Most of the activity in the public sector can be seen as service production. We end the chapter with a discussion of why innovation is also important for social welfare and human services.

Introduction

Even if we all can agree with the tribal wisdom quoted in the epigraph above, it is not easy to dismount and try to solve problems in a new and "innovative" way. Joseph Schumpeter (1883–1950) has been seen as the person who first defined and developed the concept of innovation. He was concerned with the development of the capitalist economy, and saw innovation as the engine in this development. Innovation has for most people been connected to technology and technological development, but Schumpeter (1934) had a much broader definition:

- the introduction of a new good – that is, one with which consumers are not yet familiar – or a new quality of good;
- the introduction of an improved or better method of production, which need by no means be founded upon a scientifically new discovery, or a better way of handling a commodity commercially;
- the opening of a new market – that is, a market into which the particular branch of manufacture of the country in question has not previously entered, whether or not this market has existed before;
- the discovery of a new source of supply or raw materials or half-manufactured goods, again irrespective of whether the source already existed or whether it first has to be created;

- improvements to the organization of any industry, such as the creation of monopoly position or the breaking up of a monopoly position.

The first point is what we all define as innovations – for instance, the invention of the mobile phone, and the production of it for the market, to use an example most of us are familiar with. In the market, temporary monopolies can create great profits; if they are the only ones to sell a product that people want, they can themselves set the price. After a while, they will be challenged by copycats ("karaoke capitalists") who can compete on price but are not paying back the costs of the invention and development of the product (Ridderstråle and Nordström 2004). Then there is a need for new innovations. The introduction of New Public Management (NPM), the neo-liberal model for reorganizing the public sector (Pollitt and Bouckhaert 2000; Christensen and Lægreid 2002), can illustrate Schumpeter's third point; well-known ideas from private business have been introduced into a new "market" (the public sector). According to his definition, NPM is definitely an innovation.

Although it is nearly a century since Schumpeter introduced his theory and models, the concept of innovation has only been widely used and discussed in the last few decades. It is not an easy concept to define, but in spite of some debate, there seems to be an agreement that innovation consists of two related activities, namely (1) doing something new, and (2) developing this new thing to work in a given context (Fuglsang 2010, p. 67). The first creative phase can be intentional, such as when the R&D department in a car company invents a new type of car (such as the hybrids), but it can also happen by chance, such as the discovery of penicillin. Alexander Fleming (1928) is credited with this discovery and was a researcher in the field, but it was discovered by chance because mould had grown in a Petri dish while he was on holiday. Even if a discovery happens by chance, the persons involved must be able to see the importance and potential of the "mistake", such as when 3M tried to develop an extra strong glue and found a mixture that did not work at all, but thereby invented Post-it notes. If we accept that creativity does not need to be intentional, then the implementation of discoveries does.

Today, the period between an invention and its implementation can be short, and according to capitalist logic it is important to be fast and first. However, this has not always been the case. It took more than a decade before Fleming's discovery was put into production as an effective drug. The Industrial Revolution made the twentieth century the century of innovation, because people then had the technology to realize inventions such as the aeroplane. Centuries before, Leonardo da Vinci had made drawings suggesting how a man could fly, but he had no available technology to develop his ideas further.

When new ideas are created or new discoveries made, they can supplement established knowledge in a harmonic way, but they can also challenge it. We know this from history; when it was commonly understood that the earth was flat, for instance, the discovery that it was round and moving around the sun was hard for the authorities to accept. Kuhn (1962) has proven that a process in which established knowledge has to be put aside before new knowledge can be taken into account is normal and full of conflicts.

Schumpeter states the same for innovations; often, established ways of thinking and production must be changed or destroyed before an innovation can be implemented. Schumpeter (1943) used the term "creative destruction" for this phenomenon. The term has positive connotations; we have to destroy something old and outdated to take advantage of new and better ideas or products. However, it may also go the other way, where something useful and good is superseded by something worse. This phenomenon may be labelled as "destructive creation" (Soete 2013). Some years ago, light bulbs lasted for years, reducing the need to buy new ones. Research on and implementation of new shorter-lasting light bulbs was not a positive innovation for consumers. The same is true of efforts to make software for laptops less compatible. However, these two examples may be constructive for producers, giving them better sales. It can therefore be disputed whether efforts at innovation are always universally constructive.

So far, our discussion has focused mainly on industrial products, a field many of us connect with the struggle for innovation. However, innovations can, according to Schumpeter, include other phenomena as well. NPM has already been mentioned. "Social innovations" is a relevant concept for social services (see Chapter 3). The use of methadone in the treatment of drug addicts, for instance, can be seen as an innovation. The positive effects can be fewer deaths by overdose and a reduced crime rate.

This case shows that innovation is now also a concept for the public sector and public activities. We find an equivalent division in subcategories for the public sector as the one used by Schumpeter for the private sector. Windrum (2008, p. 8) has introduced the following taxonomy:

1 service innovation
2 service delivery innovation
3 administrative and organizational innovation
4 conceptual innovation
5 policy innovation, and
6 systemic innovation.

Hartley (2005) uses some of the same categories, but also identifies strategic innovation (such as defining new goals), governance innovation (such as developing new forms of citizen or service user involvement) and rhetorical innovation (such as introducing new terminology). These categories are not mutually exclusive; the same innovation can be classified in several different categories.

We conclude this section by stating that it is common to use a wide and inclusive definition of innovation, and that we have found typologies for both the private and public sectors. However, the public sector still has to borrow taxonomies and concepts from the private sector (Hartley 2008), and the literature on innovation has been, and still is, dominated by economists (Fagerberg and Verspagen 2009).

Schumpeter died in 1950, but his work was rediscovered in the 1970s. The crisis in the world economy, during which large and international concerns got into trouble while small new businesses were established, contributed to the rediscovery. The new firms were often innovators. Not only are innovations now a must for firms that want to survive, governments are also expected to have an innovation strategy. In the EU, this strategy was introduced in the Lisbon Strategy (2000). The stated goal was to make the EU the leader in international competition by being more innovative than other countries/alliances. The strategy's lifespan was ten years, and the goals were not reached. However, the aim is still the same; innovation is still seen as the recipe for success and the magic formula for the "winners".

Innovation: imitation and adoption

"Innovate or die" can be seen a slogan for some businesses, such as the mobile phone industry. To create something new is a must for survival. However, many innovations are failures, such as the steam-powered car. These failures bring losses to the producers. It can therefore be more tempting to wait and see what the market wants, and then copy innovations developed by others ("karaoke capitalists", as mentioned above). For the public sector, for instance municipalities, it may be even more tempting to copy others, because they do not go bankrupt without innovations, and because, with a scarcity of resources, they are not inclined to run the risk of failure. Copying successes from other municipalities can be seen as responsible behaviour. However, it is not easy to imitate without innovating, even if we try. To copy a model from another organization to our own, we will need to make some adaptations because the two organizations will not be identical. If we try to copy without adjustments, a successful model in one organization can be a failure in another. From the field of sport, we know that the successful coach of one football team can be a disaster at the neighbouring team if he copies his strategy without adjustments.

Successful copying of innovations requires a qualified translator. Translators are important in organizations, in both taking up ideas from outside (on their own or as a given task) and selling them to their organization (Czarniawska and Sevon 1996). Ideas and models are filtered through the prism of some key person's understanding and interests.

When a successful innovation is tailored to a new setting, we name it an adoption. In the EU's Community Innovation Survey (CIS), imitations and adoptions are included in the operational definitions of different types of innovations. Adoptions can be more or less creative. If new elements are brought in, we can talk about a regular innovation, according to the definitions used above.

Radical and incremental innovations

In some definitions of innovation, the term is more or less reserved for radical innovations. For instance, Drejer (2004) states that innovations must be "abrupt changes that are associated with development" (p. 557). When asked to name important innovations, people will mention the light bulb, the car and other technological innovations that were a dramatic change from technological solutions used previously. These types of innovations are also called discontinuous innovations, as distinct from continuous innovations that can be seen more as improving something already in existence. However, we also have many radical organizational innovations. In the UK, the foundation of the NHS was a radical new way of organizing the health system. The public sector has seen many examples of big reorganizations. The introduction of NPM meant in some countries (New Zealand, Australia, the UK) a radical change from the past. Organizational innovations may be caused by technological ones, or they can stimulate each other. In the health and care services, new instruments and machines open up new possibilities that demand new treatments. Keyhole surgery, CT and MR are examples here. Politicians in parliaments have the power to introduce radical innovations by establishing new ministries and new laws.

Incremental innovations are small-step innovations, and seen by some authors more as changes than innovations. However, many small steps in the same direction may over time lead to radical changes, and if we go into depth and look behind a radical innovation, we will often discover that it was many small steps that made it possible to introduce this big innovation. The differences may not be that big; we should rather see incremental–radical as two poles on a scale. In the development of public services, incremental innovations can be seen as preferable. Karl Popper (1945), in his discussion of social engineering, argued for the benefit of incremental changes. With a radical reorganization of home care or human services, we will not be able to foresee all possible negative effects for service users. However, if we move forwards with small steps, we will be able to adjust our activities during the implementation process.

Services for large groups of the population provide for people with heterogeneous needs and unequal resources. An innovation may be an improvement for some groups but not for others. If that is unintended, an incremental strategy may allow for corrective action to be taken. The frequency of innovations should also be mentioned for large-scale innovations. Innovations can be seen as too frequent. Reorganizations within the school system, for instance, have consequences for parents, pupils and teachers. It will take time before a new system is understood and established. If a new model is introduced before the previous one is well established, it may cause frustration and negative attitudes towards changes (and innovations). A fair evaluation of the existing model cannot be undertaken until it is fully implemented and used.

When we include incremental innovations in our definition, we can discuss how small a change can be and still constitute an innovation. Sundbo (2008) uses the example of a hotel owner who places a fruit platter on the reception desk. For one day, it is not an innovation, but if it is repeated, it can be seen as an innovation. The argument of repetition is also mentioned by Toivonen *et al.* (2007) when they state that innovations in services must "involve some elements that can be repeated in new situations" (p. 369).

Fuglsang (2010) uses the term "bricolage" to describe small innovations that will often go under the radar of many definitions of innovation, but that are still very important in daily life. Bricolage is understood as small adjustments following a do-it-yourself principle. In an empirical study within the home care sector, Fuglsang discovered how employees used resources at hand to improve services, often to the benefit of service users. Such ad hoc adjustments can sometimes be seen as a short cut to formalized rules, but also as a way of improving practice. Bricolage is innovation at the "street level", and if leaders want to use this creativity in developing their organizations, they must be able to listen and to recognize the changes.

Innovations and improvement

The term "innovation" is often used in positively loaded sense; an innovation is something good, an improvement on what we had in the past. In a Danish text, Digmann (2010) states that something must create added value to constitute an innovation. In a scientific context, it is useful to have a more neutral understanding of the term. Furthermore, an innovation may not be to the benefit of everyone. For instance, internet banking is time-saving for many of us, but a large number of people lost their jobs in the reorganization of banking services. We may ask for whom an innovation is an improvement. In a situation with conflicting interests, an innovation may be to the benefit of one group and to the detriment of another (see Chapter 5). Innovations in the public sector will be a part of the political struggle in society. Political bodies are democratically elected to handle and regulate this struggle. In some cases, the negative consequences for a group are known in advance, activating the political resources within the group, aimed at influencing the political process in a positive way. In large-scale innovations, such as the organization of the NHS, it is not possible to know either all of the negative or all of the positive effects for service users or employees.

An innovation is seldom an end in itself; it is a means to an end. For instance, the internet made it possible for banks to reduce costs, and made banking easier for many of their customers. The criteria for evaluating innovations in a positive or negative way may vary over time and between contexts. For actors in the market, a profit is a must over time. An improved profit rate is a good measure of success, but it is not the only one; social and environmental responsibility can also be a demand.

If we take for granted that a change or innovation is not an end in itself, but only a tool for an expected improvement, it seems obvious that innovations are important in almost every organization. In many cases, we will find top-down innovations. However, improvements can also be initiated by customers or service users from the bottom up, or they may be initiated by collaborating actors. In the public sector, service users' needs should be important in deciding the criteria for success, since those defined needs are the main reason for establishing the services (school, elderly care, etc.).

To conclude, we must differentiate between an innovation and an improvement. An innovation does not need to be an improvement, and an improvement does not need to be an innovation.

Innovations and tacit knowledge

Export and copying of innovations presupposes that the "recipe" can be conveyed. Then it has to be articulated, and normally codified either in letters or numbers. However, for organizational innovations, much of the knowledge may be an unarticulated part of the culture. The actors may not even be aware of it. Knowledge that can be articulated can be transferred. If it can be digitized, it can easily be globalized. For instance, a doctor in the US can send his X-rays to India when he leaves the office and get them interpreted back in the morning. Tacit knowledge is connected to the people who have it, and can be transferred from them. The old system with master and apprentice made this transfer possible. The best violins, for instance, were constructed by masters in late middle age, such as Antonio Stradivarius (1648–1737) (Dreyfus and Dreyfus 1986). These masters had learned from their masters, and probably developed new skills in addition. It has so far not been possible to produce the same quality in factories. As regards innovations, the advice will be to visit and spend time in the organization we want to learn from. We can then observe what we find that is different from our own setting. This way of learning limits the spread of knowledge, compared to what could be done with codified knowledge in books or lessons given to large groups (Asheim and Gertler 2005; Behn 2008). Tacit knowledge is a challenge if external actors come into an organization to conduct an innovation, since they only have access to the codified knowledge. From organizational theory, we know that informal structures can both support and undermine the formal ones (Chan 2002).

In a discussion of knowledge production, Gibbons *et al.* (1994) differentiate between two different forms, labelled as Mode 1 and Mode 2. Mode 1 is the traditional specialized production of knowledge within scientific disciplines. Here all knowledge is supposed to be articulated. In Mode 2, knowledge is transdisciplinary, picked pragmatically from several fields. Knowledge embodied in people with emphasis on the tacit component can take precedence over codified knowledge, and established knowledge can be a hindrance for problem-solving rather than a support. In some projects aimed at innovative activity, Mode 2 has proved to be preferable. With empirical support from Japanese industry, Takeuchi and Nonaka (1986) have argued for a holistic approach, in which the actors behave as a rugby team, more than as a relay team. The different competencies have to be brought together in real time. Both doers and thinkers are needed. Tacit knowledge is still seen as important.

The importance of context

Context can here be defined as "situational opportunities and constraints that affect the occurrence and meaning of organizational behaviour as well as functional relationships between variables" (Johns 2006, quoted by Bamberger 2008, p. 839).

A successful model for reorganizing a branch of the public sector is always grounded in a particular setting. Two municipalities will not be identical; they are a product of their own history, traditions and structures, and of the people who work or have worked there. In the evaluation of innovation competitions in the UK (the Beacon Scheme), it has been pinpointed that there are problems in copying innovations (Hartley 2008). As mentioned above, successful innovations are suited to the structures in which they are implemented, and therefore they have to be adapted to the structures to which they are exported. The regimes described by Esping-Andersen (1990) will offer different contexts for welfare deliveries, and be favourable to different ways of organizing them. Several case studies support the statement that innovation in public sector services clearly takes place in a specific context of government and governance, which makes it different from private sector innovation (Fuglsang and Rønning 2014).

There is an understanding in many countries that some places seem to have more creative people than others. If creativity is seen as a must for innovation and survival in the market, then hunting for creative people will be important. Florida (2002) has stated that this struggle to attract the "creative class" will be important for the development of business activities and public support in the future. He has also argued (2008) that where to live is the most important decision of your life; you are where you live. Innovations will flourish in metropolitan areas. Growth and prosperity will occur in the large, heterogeneous and creative regions. Contrary to this hypothesis, however, it can be argued that, since knowledge that can be codified and digitized can easily be disseminated around the world, the problem of distance can be eliminated. Friedman (2006) therefore concludes that you do not need to emigrate to innovate. In line with this reasoning, Nordstrøm and Ridderstråle (1999) proclaim that "the new immigrants will be virtual ones, taking jobs from someone else without even showing their faces" (p. 45).

Innovation and causality

In many contexts, it is regarded as important to institutionalize an innovation that is seen as an improvement, either within that organization or as a model to be used by others. It is then important to understand which activities or mechanisms have made the innovation successful. However, it is sometimes difficult to prove a causal relationship. From manuals on methods, we know that we should be able to falsify all correlations other than the one we trust. In practice, in complex structures, that will seldom be possible. If we start two activities (x and y) to get our wanted improvement (I), and we get I, it is tempting to claim that x and y caused I, and to sell this as the recipe. However, many other influences are possible; we can, for instance, have an observer effect. That is not uncommon in intervention programmes for targeted groups. In private firms, boards wanting to encourage well-paid managers to exceed targets and expectations can offer bonuses if the results go up. However, both bad and good results may be caused by factors out of the control of the managers. For the CEO of an oil company, for instance, a war in the Middle East would inflate prices, but in most cases the CEO would not have contributed to start it.

Innovation in (public) services: our understanding is lagging behind

In the industrial society, the production of goods was essential. The Industrial Revolution was founded on access to energy and machinery for mass production. Today, services represent the major part of the economy in developed countries. In the US, services now engage 80 per cent of the workforce, and some European countries are more or less in the same situation (Rubalcaba and Di Meglio 2009). Adam Smith saw services as non-productive, but he died in 1790. Even today, some central actors are reluctant to accept services as productive. The former French president Nicolas Sarkozy said, while he was Minister of Finance, that "[W]e need a strong French manufacturing industry .... France cannot be only an economy of banks, insurances and services" (France Info 2004). Some years ago, there was a boom in the estimated value of IT companies. Then, the slogan was the opposite of Sarkozy's statement; if you can touch it, it does not count (Ridderstråle and Nordstrøm 2008). Even if services are now generally recognized as the dominant part of the economy, many economists complain that models and the use of indicators and statistics are lagging behind. These are still not tailored to service production (Rubalcaba 2007; Gallouj and Toivonen 2011).

In contracting out home care services, we also find some elements of the traditional production model. In Nordic countries, the procedure is that service users are placed in a limited number of categories, from those with the greatest need for assistance to those with the least. Normally six to eight categories are used. All of the service users within the same category are supposed to have the same needs, and they will be given the same service. When the service level for each category is defined, and the number in each category is given, the municipalities can open a competitive bidding process. This way of treating a tender sees care as something that can be defined in advance, as a standardized good that the provider owns and can sell to municipalities and give to service users. However, care can be defined as "taking the role of the other" (Noddings 1984), which means that the carer must be open to the needs expressed by the care receiver, or what can be observed as an obvious need. Predefined care is a contradiction, following this definition. Good care cannot easily be standardized; every service user has to be seen as unique. In addition, care-giving is a service, not an exchange of goods, and services are created in collaboration with the receiver, rather than being predefined.

Services can be defined in many ways. Hill (1977) has a much-used definition: "A service is a change in the condition of a person or a good belonging to some economic unit, which results from the activity of another economic unit, with the agreement of the former" (p. 318). A service is not necessarily tangible, often you cannot store or transport it, production and consumption or use cannot be separated, and it is based on a relation between giver and receiver (Rubalcaba 2007). What we often label as the "service sector" encompasses quite different activities such as trade, transport, the production and exchange of knowledge, health and care services, tourism and telecommunications. There are differences and similarities between these activities. The definition of services will change because the content of services changes, and it may be wise not to use a static definition (Rubalcaba and Di Meglio 2009). We can differentiate between a logic of goods, in which physical resources, products and systems are important, and a logic of services, in which competence, capabilities and motivation among employees are important (Vargo and Lusch 2004). Some authors focus on the differences between these two logics, while others see the similarities (Sundbo 2002). However, there are obvious connections, such as when we buy a good with connected services. Often it will be the experience we get, not the product itself, that matters, such as when we buy a stereo with high-quality sound.

It is important to note that for a service, the value is created when the service user or customer experiences it. Users are co-creators of a service; the content depends on the receiver. In teaching, for instance, the content of a lecture for a student will depend on how well prepared they are, and how active they are in listening and in asking questions. In home care, the interaction between the care giver and the care receiver is important. Did the receiver manage to express their needs and wishes, and did the giver manage to understand them and react adequately? Many other factors can influence the experience of receiving care, such as the receiver's background and attitudes. A service is not given before it is received. How active the user is, and is expected to be, in the co-creation of the service varies for different types of services, and it varies for different users. If you take a dancing course, or go to a speech therapist, for instance, you are supposed to be active. Going to the hairdresser demands less from the customer, and indeed being too active can cause problems for the service provider.

"Co-creation" sounds like a positively loaded term to most of us; we create something together and the customer or service user gets some added value. However, it may not always be so constructive. Many unemployed people, living on social assistance, visit advisors to get help to get a job. They can need positive feedback and improved self-confidence to handle their situation. The encounter may be a positive interaction, after which the service user leaves the office with a positive attitude and a belief that he or she can manage to get back into work. However, there are other outcomes. The service user can leave with a feeling of having been humiliated, with less self-confidence and unable to see a way out of his or her situation. In this case, the interaction has been destructive, and the service experience can be seen as a "co-destruction" (Echeverri and Skålen 2011).

In discussing care above, individualized treatment was said to be a condition for good care. This is valid for other services as well, such as hairdressing. However, in service businesses we find a mix between standardized services and tailored services. For instance, we can go with a big group to the Canary Islands for a holiday, or we can opt for an exclusive trip to Nepal. We can eat at a burger bar, or in an expensive restaurant. The price level varies, and some groups can only afford a package holiday to the Canaries, while others can afford the exclusive offers. However, many people like to use both ends of the service scale; they take a low-cost flight to Rome but stay in an exclusive hotel, and so on. Some low-cost services leave more of the job to the customers; we fill the car ourselves at the petrol station, pay the bills on the internet and clear our table at the burger bar. The term "McDonaldization" has been used to describe standardized low-cost services in which the customers do a part of the job (Ritzer 1998).

For social welfare and human services, we also find standardized services, such as when the unemployed register and apply for new jobs on the internet. There will probably be continuous debate about what can be expected of service users. Here it is difficult to standardize; some elderly people manage, and want to do as much as they can, while others seem unable to handle simple tasks. How much should they be helped, and how much should they be pushed? The problem is well known from home carers' interactions with widowers. How helpless should they be accepted to be in the kitchen? There is a demand for equal treatment in public services when the receivers do not pay full price for the service. The introduction of the internet in communication with service users also triggers discussions about the service user interface. The rules here have to be dynamic because the level of competence among service users will increase over time. Expectations have to be different for different groups of recipients of public assistance. Retired people in their nineties cannot be expected (as a norm) to use the internet, while it may be reasonable to expect young unemployed people to do so.

We find, as mentioned, standardized elements in both health and welfare services. However, most of these services are by nature based on individualized treatment. Psychologists, doctors, dentists and speech therapists cannot in any meaningful way standardize the core of their services. Unlike the production of goods, human services cannot be conducted by machines; they have to be conducted by people through social interactions.

We conclude this section by underlining that the public sector must be treated as a service producer, and that we need adequate models to discuss and understand these activities in general, especially if we want to engage in innovations in the sector. This will be discussed further in Chapter 4.

Why innovations are needed in social welfare and human services

We end this chapter with a discussion about the need for innovation in these services. It does not seem to be obvious for all actors in the field that they should engage in innovative work in their field, or in innovations in general. Judging by the number of textbooks and relevant journal papers published, innovation is still not a hot topic in the field. This is very different from the health services, in which strong drivers have pushed for both technological and medical innovations, which also create a need for organizational innovations.

We encounter two viewpoints that prevent people from engaging in innovative work in their field. One is that innovation is merely a popular phenomenon – a fashionable trend or fad – and will soon be replaced by a new trend. In the private sector, innovation has been important as a competitive force for 50 years now, and the need for new solutions to given tasks are also obvious in the public sector. To wait until the "trend" has passed is not a viable option.

The second viewpoint is that innovation is merely a new word for an activity they have been conducting for years, because they are continuously improving their services. It is true that many people in the field engage in this type of work, and that some of their activities can be labelled either as bricolage or incremental innovations. However, not all changes are innovations. Development along established lines is a well-known recipe for change, but not an innovation. Our definition of innovation has two components; the first is to create something new, and the second is to implement it. Public employees have much experience in implementing political decisions, but probably less experience as innovators, since they have been in organizations with a tradition of top-down control. Our conclusion, then, is that many people in welfare services have been engaged in improving services, but that they are not very familiar with creative processes aimed at reorganizing their service in a completely new way.

In general, we argue that an organization that worked well yesterday does not work well today if it has not tried to improve the way it operates, because the environment will have changed. As Chairman Mao famously commented, "You cannot go two times into the same river".

The imperatives for continuous development are specified below.

Environmental changes

Behaviour that was quite reasonable when it was initiated can after some time appear to be less so. The public sector has to adapt to changes in the private sector, and the private sector has to adapt to innovations initiated by public authorities (such as the internet). *Technological development* is a very visible driver, influencing our activities, human relations and the relation between welfare services and their users. Many new treatments for deadly diseases are available; patients with chronic diseases get much information from the internet and expect their GP to be up-to-date. Mobile phones and internet services make us accessible day and night, and this challenges us as individuals and as professional workers. Rules and behaviour have to be adapted.

Economic development also influences our life and lifestyles. Poverty is often defined in a relative way, as a percentage below median income. We still have poverty in developed countries in spite of the rising wealth of large groups. Some time ago, the poor did not get enough nutrition and food. Today, they get enough food in developed countries, but not necessarily healthy food. In 2010, the Mayor of New York proposed that people receiving food stamps should not be allowed to buy food containing much sugar, because he wanted to fight obesity. Obesity is now a huge health problem in the developed world, causing diabetes, heart problems and many other ailments. Two generations ago, campaigns for better hygiene were important for improving public health; today, campaigns are targeting obesity in many countries.

Political changes will also challenge established solutions. Politicians can be seen as selling new (and better) solutions to known and so-called "wicked problems" (Australian Public Service Commission 2007). The neo-liberal wave of the late 1970s, represented by politicians such as Margaret Thatcher and Ronald Reagan, brought ideas from the private sector into public services. Thatcher said that "there is no such thing as society" (1987) and Reagan concluded that "government is not the solution, government is the problem" (Levitan and Johnson 1984). Both quotations express the view that people's problems are not a public responsibility. "Big government" had to be reduced and NPM was the recipe. The task was seen as very challenging:

> our governments are like fat people who must lose weight. They need to eat less and exercise more; instead, when money is tight they cut off a few fingers and toes. *To melt the fat, we must change the basic incentives that drive our governments.* We must turn bureaucratic institutions into entrepreneurial institutions, ready to kill off obsolete initiatives, willing to do more for less, eager to absorb new ideas.
>
> (Osborne and Gaebler 1993, p. 23, emphasis in original)

NPM was an innovation in the public sector, but was not necessarily seen as an improvement by all actors. All of the nations that tried to realize the new ideas developed their own version of it. New Zealand has been seen as the country that tried to realize the most clear-cut NPM regime (Christensen and Lægreid 2007). Treating the users of public services as customers gave more attention to their needs. More service user involvement was also stimulated by other movements in society, such as the formation of patient groups. Disabled people organized into an "independent living" movement, demanding support from society to live as independently as they could. The establishment of a system with user-controlled personal assistants was seen as a solution and an innovation; disabled people got support for hiring assistants of whom they were in charge.

More of the same does not work

Sometimes, we have to conclude that a treatment does not have the expected effects, or that the effects are too limited with respect to the costs. If, for instance, we are working to rehabilitate people and yet few successful rehabilitations take place, it may be time for a period of reflection and innovation.

We should keep in mind that interventions to solve problems in welfare services are based on an understanding of a causal chain. Professionals will have models here, but politicians may have a different understanding. If we take sickness absence as an example, we can see that the dominant and hegemonic explanations have changed. A Swedish study, based on content analysis of newspaper data (Johnsson 2010), concludes that the trade unions' view of sickness absence as caused by a more brutal labour market dominated public opinion from 2000 to 2001. Later, the view that people were exploiting a too generous system became dominant. If politicians find the expenditure on sickness absence benefits to be too high, the cure will be quite different depending on which of the two views they believe in. In the first case, it will be reasonable to regulate the labour market; in the latter, a more restrictive public support system will be an appropriate medicine. Innovations are needed, but the premises for the work will be different. The more restricted a support system is, the less it will be exploited – but the possibility of denying support to people who genuinely need it will increase. In our laws, we have decided that it is worse to punish someone who is innocent than to release someone who is guilty. The prosecutors have to prove that the accused are guilty, not the other way around. This is a decision about prioritizing values. When we come to welfare services, it is not obvious that the same principle should be used. Politicians will have different opinions about who deserves to get public support, and a decision to innovate may be triggered by these opinions and a change in values on the part of the dominant actors. Since politics is about prioritizing the use of available resources, costs and the need for a more efficient organization of services can always be an argument for innovation.

Knowledge about the negative effects of what we have done

As mentioned above, a radical innovation may cause negative effects that were not foreseen at the outset. If these negative effects are considered to be sufficiently serious and unacceptable by the decision-makers, the project can be stopped. Another solution is to try to modify the project to minimize the negative effects. Sometimes, the negative effects are seen as unavoidable and part of the price. If the government wants to build a new highway, for instance, some houses will often have to be destroyed, together with arable land. When the child welfare authorities decide to take a child away from his or her parents, it will also be a balancing act between positive and negative effects. Introducing programmes for the vaccination of large groups of the population will be based on similar calculations; the vaccines have to be tested in advance. The crucial question is how many will be saved from a serious illness, in relation to the expected number of negative side-effects. The expected pandemic of swine flu triggered a fast reaction from health authorities in many countries. Later, unexpected negative side-effects were discovered, as a significant number of people got narcolepsy, probably caused by the vaccines.

In medicine, there are established norms for documentation before a new medicine is introduced, and calculations according to established criteria do not leave much to the decision-makers' discretion. However, in many other fields the weighing of costs against positive effects is dependent on the subjective discretion of the decision-makers.

Conclusion

We end this chapter by stating that people have always innovated, mostly driven by a desire to make the future better than the present. The inventions of the wheel, the engine, antibiotics, and so on have made it easier for people to manage everyday life. However, inventions – when implemented to be innovations – can also have also a dark side; we call these "destructive creations". We mentioned earlier the research into reducing the lifespan of light bulbs. That can be seen as a "harmless" example, compared to the energy used to develop more cruel instruments for torture, or the scientific efforts to exterminate groups of people (such as the Jews in the Second World War).

However, not every change is an innovation, as defined in this book. We need to do something new. In spite of the fact that large innovations occur unintentionally, we should not trust in this randomness. Both in Fleming's case and others, it was necessary for competent people to recognize that randomness as serendipitous and to take advantage of it. It is a challenge in social welfare and human services to stimulate innovative activities. The actors need to be open-minded, and a starting point must be that it is always possible to solve a problem in a new (and improved) way.

The development of the ICEHOTEL in Jukkasjärvi in the north of Sweden (www.icehotel.com) can be an example. The founder, Yngve Bergkvist, was not satisfied with his business and was reflecting on opportunities to create something new. Located far away from metropolitan areas, and without access to known and valuable natural resources, he found that Jukkasjärvi had a long winter and water from the Torne River to provide a plentiful supply of clean, unpolluted ice. Inspired by Japanese ice artists, he decided to build an ice hotel. It has been a success. Not only is Jukkasjärvi now a spot on the tourist maps, but they export ice to ice pubs in big cities in the Western world. We should never rest on our laurels.

3   Social innovation

A diffuse concept?

We can't solve problems by using the same kind of thinking we used when we created them.

(Albert Einstein, quoted by Harris 1995)

This chapter highlights the often vaguely defined but widely popular concept of social innovation. The purpose of this chapter is to problematize its meaning, highlighting the different definitions, to point out the importance of social innovation processes, and to critically analyse expectations and confidence in social innovation as a solution to society's problems. Terms such as "social innovation", "social entrepreneurship" and "social enterprise" are often seen in a positive way. There is a confusion between these terms, and sometimes they are used interchangeably. An underlying reason for this is the lack of clarity surrounding definitions of diffuse concepts such as social innovation. One ambition of this chapter is to sort out some of this confusion.

Introduction

In order to tackle the problems that have been caused by our old way of thinking, we need a new way of thinking (see the epigraph above). Even though a shift of mindset is necessary for change, we also need new ways of organizing. Since the financial crisis of 2008, we have witnessed a large wave and global spread of citizens' protests such as the 15-M Movement, Occupy Wall Street and the Arab Spring (Casero-Ripollés and Feenstra 2012; Philip and Hussain 2011). These movements have used social media and more specifically mobile phones as a way of organizing and communicating. Photos and videos were uploaded on YouTube and Facebook, and issues were debated on Twitter. The mobile phone is a technological innovation, but has led to social innovations and to the socio-political mobilization and empowerment of people (Hulgård and Shajahan 2013; Casero-Ripollés and Feenstra 2012). These recent trends show the importance of theorizing social innovation in order to understand what is really going on. Mulgan (2012) has argued that the field of social innovation "has been led by practice rather than theory" (p. 19). That is true for all innovations; they have a practical purpose – namely, to change something for the better (for someone). However, theoretical studies can also be useful. In relation to social innovation, social movement theories and neo-institutional theories are useful. As we can see in the above example, social movements can be the result of people striving for democracy and social justice, and therefore these struggles are a matter of empowerment and political engagement. Research on social innovations should engage with the concept of power. Social innovations can thus create conditions that give voice to groups of people who do not usually get their voices heard in the media or in the political system (Moulaert *et al.* 2005). The term "social" is used in quite different contexts, and sometimes as a generic term for everything that is not technological. In this sense, organizational innovations are social. In this chapter, we focus on social innovation as a solution to the current social and environmental challenges that humanity is facing: poverty, ageing populations, health problems, climate change, water and food insecurity, etc. Let us first highlight some definitions of this convoluted concept.

What is social innovation?

At first glance, it may appear that the concept of social innovation is only a fad. However, while the term can be seen as a buzzword, we can trace the roots back to Schumpeter's (1943) concept of creative destruction (see Chapter 2). Some authors have suggested that James Taylor first coined the term in 1970 in his article *Introducing Social Innovation*, while others trace it back to the revolts in Europe during the 1960s (Moulaert *et al.* 2013; Jessop *et al.* 2013). The term "social innovation" can be seen as a semantic magnet (Bergmark *et al.* 2011, p. 152). This means that it has a magnetic ability to attract a number of meanings. The term also has a positive charge, making it difficult for anyone to say that they are against social innovation. It is also a political term. How social innovations are defined is highly significant. A narrow definition of the term excludes certain innovations, while too broad a definition will include almost anything. When an overly broad definition is applied, it is difficult to determine what distinguishes social innovations from social change where, for example, an organization implements improvements in a particular service to become more cost-effective. Here are some examples of how the term "social innovation" has been defined:

- "A novel solution to a social problem that is more effective, efficient, sustainable, or just than existing solutions and for which the value created accrues primarily to society as a whole rather than private individuals" (Phills *et al.* 2008, p. 36).
- "Social innovations are innovations that are social in both their ends and their means. Specifically, we define social innovations as new ideas (products, services and models) that simultaneously meet social needs (more effectively than alternatives) and create new social relationships or

collaborations. They are innovations that are not only good for society but also enhance society's capacity to act" (Hubert 2010, p. 7). (This is the definition that the EU Commission uses.)

- "[…] the generation and implementation of new ideas about how people should organize interpersonal activities, or social interactions, to meet one or more common goals" (Mumford 2002, p. 253).
- "[…] the generation and implementation of new social-service ideas for solving social problems" (Svensson and Bengtsson 2010, p. 192).
- "[…] new, more effective and/or more efficient social practices with social ends and social means" (Franz *et al.* 2012, p. 6).
- "[…] fostering inclusion and wellbeing through improving social relations and empowerment processes: imagining and pursuing a world, a nation, a region, a locality, a community that would grant universal rights and be more socially inclusive" (Moulaert *et al.* 2013, p. 16).

Some recurring ingredients in these definitions of the term "social innovation", which also tally with the ingredients that we discussed in Chapter 2 as part of the definition of innovation in general, are that it should be:

- something new;
- better than available solutions;
- good for society in general.

Social innovations can thus be both processes and products, but it is important that these are better than the existing products or processes. The criterion that an innovation should be something new does not mean that it must be a completely new idea; the idea can be borrowed from another context and thus become new in a new setting, for a new service user, or in how it is applied (Phills *et al.* 2008, p. 37). The innovation should also be good for society in general. This normative aspect is, of course, complicated. Who will benefit from the social innovation and who have the power to formulate what is good for society? What is important for the argument of this book is that how social innovations are defined matters. Recent research on social innovations has identified different strands. On the one hand, there is a strand that focuses on social innovations as a means of fostering solidarity and empowerment. On the other hand, social innovations are seen as a solution to the most urgent problems facing marginalized groups (Klein 2013). "Social innovation" is a broad and unstable term, and as such its meaning tends to be constantly renegotiated.

Different authors have suggested many varying examples of social innovations. Mumford and Moertl (2003) highlight the International Monetary Fund (IMF) and the Scouting movement. IMF may not be the most obvious example of a social innovation, but, based on the authors' reasoning, it is an example of how new industries, policies or institutions are created. Mulgan (2006) argues that the Wikipedia, The Open University, so-called "carbon-free housing developments" and self-help groups on the internet are all examples of social innovations. Phills *et al.* (2008) propose microfinance, Supported Employment and Fair Trade as examples of contemporary social innovations.

Social innovation should also be seen as a political concept. Within social science research, this becomes evident at the EU level, where the new EU framework programme Horizon 2020, the Framework Programme for Research and Innovation, very clearly highlights innovation as a central concept. The European Platform against Poverty and Social Exclusion (EC 2010) uses the concept of evidence-based social innovation. The platform states that innovations should only have a bearing on the basis of a social policy perspective and that they should be grounded in evidence, the best possible available knowledge. The concept of evidence-based innovation is something of a paradox; an innovation should be something new, while evidence is about knowing if the innovation will have the intended impact. In this perspective, the political dimension of the concept becomes clear. Innovations that have been shown to have an effect on poverty and social exclusion should be diffused, according to the EU. It is important to recognize the significance of context; even if an innovation has proven to be fruitful and successful in one context, it does not mean that this will be the case in a new setting. When does an innovation stop being innovative if we imagine that it should also be evidence-based? On the one hand, social innovations are path-dependent, but, in order for them to be scaled up and have a more systemic impact, Martinelli (2012) argues that they should "acquire a relatively *durable* character and become an *embedded societal acquisition* that can last beyond the initial mobilisation/innovation moment and until the next round of innovation" (p. 172, emphasis in original). The term "social innovation", as well as other terms, tends to have a strong impact since it is connected to major funding programmes for research and development. This means that the phenomenon's actual application is secondary to its presence in project applications. Further proof of the EU's interest in social innovations, apart from the Horizon 2020 programme, is the establishment of so-called "hubs". A hub means the central point that unites a network. The term is now also used for other types of networks. The latest hub is Social Innovation Europe (SIE, www.socialinnovationeurope.eu). SIE can be described as a virtual meeting place.

If we carefully examine the concept of social innovation, we find that it is not only about creating new innovative solutions. There is a clear link to "new forms of organisation and interactions to tackle social issues" (Hubert 2010, p. 26). Social innovations thus have a clear connection to social problems, and the challenge for socially innovative activities is to solve, or to help to solve, these problems. Another perspective is to assume that there is a range of solutions just waiting for the right problems to emerge (Cohen *et al.* 1972).

The street newspaper movement as a social innovation

Let us take *The Big Issue* as an example. *The Big Issue* is a street newspaper launched in 1991 in London by John Bird and Gordon Roddick. Roddick picked up the inspiration for a street magazine from the street newspaper *Street News* in

New York. It is not easy to pinpoint what it is that is innovative about *The Big Issue*. In a sense, the very idea of a street newspaper was innovative when *Street News* began its operations. For *The Big Issue*, the idea of a street newspaper was innovative since it was organized as a business. In this way, *The Big Issue* can be seen as an organizational innovation. From a historical perspective, however, street newspapers are nothing new. In the book *Print Culture in a Diverse America*, Adrian (1998) describes *The Hobo News* as the 1910s version of today's street newspapers. One feature common to the street newspapers that have emerged since the 1980s is that they have a role in trying to raise public awareness of social problems by providing an alternative voice on issues that the mainstream media ignores or misses (Heinz 2004; Parlette 2010; Torck 2001; Howley 2003). From a historical perspective, this is something that today's street newspapers share with other journals such as *The Hobo News*. Street newspapers as a phenomenon can thus not be seen as something new.

The Big Issue is, however, often described as an example of a social innovation. Street newspapers are a response to the homeless and other marginalized groups in society who have difficulty entering the labour market. Selling copies of a street newspaper makes the homeless self-employed and enables self-help. In order to become vendors, individuals have to prove that they are homeless. Then they undergo a short period of training and sign an agreement on how they should behave. After completing the training, vendors get an identification card that they must carry while selling on the street. The principle is simple – vendors buy magazines for a sum from the distributor and then sell them on for double the price. The vendors keep the difference. However, it is not only the legitimate revenues that are a win for vendors. An increased self-esteem and sense of inclusion are also described as key ingredients in the business model (Swithinbank 2001; Hanks and Swithinbank 1997, p. 149).

The Big Issue is a for-profit business that receives its funding through sales of magazines and through advertisements. This form of organization means that the magazine is not dependent on municipal grants or other charitable funds. The emergence and spread of street newspapers since the 1990s reveals that social innovation processes often involve many smaller changes, called incremental changes (see Chapter 2), rather than major revolutionary changes (radical innovations). *The Big Issue* quickly became a commercial success and spread internationally. Although *Street News* can be considered the first modern-day street newspaper, it is the particular concept behind *The Big Issue* that has spread in Europe because of its business principles (Hanks and Swithinbank 1997; Magnusson 2002; Swärd 2004). This diffusion process is interesting from an innovation perspective.

The two street newspapers represent two different models; *The Big Issue* represents a business model while *Street News* represents a so-called representative model (Magnusson 2002, p. 16; Lindemann 2007). The business model means that the newspaper is run as a social enterprise that has to break even and be sustainable, without being dependent on, for example, grants from government, foundations, local businesses and the like. In the business model, professional journalists and editors are responsible for the content and production of the newspaper. In the representation model, homeless people themselves produce the newspaper and also try to write about important issues in the homelessness debate from their own perspective. Magnusson (2002) argues that street newspapers have a paradoxical function since they are both a commercial enterprise, in that the newspaper is sold for profit, and at the same time have the organizational goal of helping the homeless. They thus resemble both a voluntary organization and a private company (Magnusson 2002, p. 15). Hanks and Swithinbank (1997) note that one of the unique characteristics of *The Big Issue* as compared to *Street News* is that the former is not based on the principle of charity. Magnusson (2002) argues that the majority of street newspaper organizations are based on the principle of helping people to help themselves. An important difference is that the content of *The Big Issue* and other subsequent street newspapers that were created to follow a business-driven model is intended to be of interest to a broader public. These newspapers can therefore not only address issues of homelessness. *The Big Issue* had to adapt to the environment in order to attract public interest. New organizations that followed emulated *The Big Issue* as a successful business model. The spread of street newspapers around the world showed in many ways how these new organizations copied and emulated the already existing structures of other street newspapers.

The social innovation process

Social innovations occur in a number of different types of organizations, both within the public sector and voluntary organizations and in companies in the private sector. Murray *et al.* (2010) argue that it is primarily in the space between the civil, family, business and public spheres that the social economy exists, and it is within this market that social innovations are mainly formed (Wijkström and Einarsson 2006, p. 21). In this book, we focus primarily on the innovations that take shape within organizations that provide social and welfare services. According to Murray *et al.* (2010), the social innovation process differs from that of commercial innovations in the private sector. They argue that it is problematic to transfer different business models and practices to the social sphere without translation and adaptation to the local context. The social innovation process can be divided into six stages:

1 prompts, inspirations and diagnoses
2 proposals and ideas
3 prototyping and pilots
4 sustaining
5 scaling and diffusion
6 systemic change.

(Murray *et al.* 2010, pp. 12–13)

Research is often used to call attention to social problems that need to be addressed, and an idea becomes the first driver of the creation of a new innovation. Necessity is often the mother of invention. A crisis triggers an immediate need to find solutions to handle the situation, such as when a natural disaster quickly requires new forms of solutions. It is a common feature of these solutions that they are of little use when the immediate crisis is over. This is one of the reasons why many charity organizations provide acute solutions for very pressing needs.

The innovation process of the street newspaper movement could be described as follows. There was a need for change, since there was a rise in homelessness in Britain from the end of the 1980s. The idea that the homeless could sell a magazine fitted in well with the changing political climate that was behind the introduction of NPM. Street newspapers came to fill an identified gap in welfare. At the same time, there was also an underlying idea that homeless people should work instead of begging. To sell newspapers was to be employed instead of being dependent on welfare.

John Bird can be seen as an expert by experience, since he had a long experience of both homelessness and of different forms of institutions. This was an important source of knowledge. Gordon Roddick had been inspired by the street newspaper idea from contacts with newspaper vendors in the US. He also brought in experience from being a chairman of The Body Shop, which contributed to how the *The Big Issue* was shaped as an organization (Magnusson 2002). During the birth of the organization, a number of problems and mistakes were made and resolved, mistakes that many of the subsequent street newspapers did not have to repeat.

Nowadays, street newspapers are a common feature in many European cities. The social innovation has, in other words, both been scaled up and disseminated. How social innovations spread is a very interesting research area, but perhaps more important for the social innovation process is whether social innovations can be considered to have contributed to some form of major systemic change – a change in the prevailing human behaviours, values or structures. This is debatable (see Alvord *et al.* 2004). Hanks and Swithinbank (1997) argue that it is difficult to know what happens to vendors over time. Some have taken up university studies and others have received various types of work. Any vendor who goes from being homeless and sleeping rough to having a job tends to be exploited as a success story. There are plenty of good examples of people who get themselves out of difficult situations and into leading a completely different life. However, while it is easy to identify individual success stories as a result of social innovation, it is much harder to identify changes that affect the overall structures such as durable categorical inequalities that contribute to social exclusion in society. This has also prompted criticism that street newspapers' self-help ideology tends to individualize structural problems. Success stories have a central role within this ideology. In a Swedish context, Per Holknekt – the founder of the clothing company Odd Molly – came to symbolize the potential journey ("from rough sleeper to designer") for a street newspaper vendor (Swärd 2004, p. 277). When an innovation is directed towards individuals, it is evident that one cannot expect it to have an effect on institutional structures.

However, it is possible that improvements for individual street newspaper vendors can contribute to spread the phenomenon of street newspapers and that these organizations can provide an alternative voice and a different picture of homelessness than the mainstream media. In this sense, it is possible that organizations can influence and change public perceptions of homelessness. In this case, the innovation reaches beyond an individual vendor's financial and social situation. The example of *The Big Issue* can thus elucidate how innovations at one level can affect and have an impact at other levels. From a policy perspective, it is important to connect the different levels. Interventions at a national level will have different effects at the local level, where local policy-making is of importance. Innovations that create systemic change affect all spheres – the civil sphere, the family sphere, the business sphere and the governmental sphere. The welfare state, say Murray *et al.* (2010), is one example. It often requires some form of shift of mindset and, above all, a new way of organizing. This leads to changes in, among other things, power relations (Murray *et al.* 2010, p. 107). The criticism of street newspapers can be transferred to social innovation as a phenomenon. The popularity of social innovations can be seen as part of a neo-liberal trend in which they become tools to stimulate the social economy to create new jobs in new markets. Within the neo-liberal discourse, social services need to be privatized in order to downsize a bureaucratic welfare state (Moulaert *et al.* 2005).

We have used *The Big Issue* to demonstrate how a social innovation can manifest itself and how the social innovation process can be understood. In the next section, we will discuss how social innovation relates to social entrepreneurship and social enterprise.

Social enterprises, social entrepreneurship and social innovation

In this section, we will briefly attempt to distinguish between social innovation, social entrepreneurship and social enterprises. To fully clarify the differences between these terms requires a thorough historical and conceptual investigation, since both social entrepreneurship and social enterprises tend to be equally fuzzy terms. To make such a thorough investigation lies beyond the scope of our book. Instead, we will use concrete examples to try to point out the differences between the concepts and thus demonstrate the importance of making a distinction between them. Social innovation, according to Svensson and Bengtsson (2010, p. 191), is seen as the core of social entrepreneurship. Phills *et al.* (2008) make a distinction between social enterprises, social entrepreneurs and social innovation. They argue that it is the latter that we should focus on to identify effective mechanisms that lead to social change. Often it seems as if social entrepreneurship is merely equated with social innovations (Alvord *et al.* 2004).

A social business is, according to Yunus (2010), "a non-loss, non-dividend company with a social objective" (p. 4). Yunus also believes that the mission of these businesses is "solving social, economic, and environmental problems that have long plagued humankind – hunger, homelessness, disease, pollution, igno-rance" (p. vii). Social businesses are often confused with corporate social responsibility (CSR) (Borglund *et al.* 2008). This means that profit-maximizing firms are making investments that show that they have adopted CSR. Through CSR, companies can build up their reputation and thereby obtain legitimacy within the organizational field. These investments need not have anything to do with social entrepreneurship, according to Yunus' definition above; on the con-trary, it is either philanthropic contributions or investments to help to solve a social problem. A co-operative is also a form of organization that tends to be confused with a social enterprise.

Bornstein and Davis (2010) argue that social entrepreneurship "is a process by which citizens build or transform institutions to advance solutions to social problems, such as poverty, illness, illiteracy, environmental destruction, human rights abuses and corruption, in order to make life better for many" (p. 1). The definition of social entrepreneurship shows that even this term has been vaguely defined. Martin and Osberg (2007) seek to distinguish the social entrepreneur from activists and those who provide social services. A social entrepreneur is someone

> who targets an unfortunate but stable equilibrium that causes the neglect, marginalization, or suffering of a segment of humanity; who brings to bear on this situation his or her inspiration, direct action, creativity, courage, and fortitude; and who aims for and ultimately affects the establishment of a new stable equilibrium that secures permanent benefit for the targeted group and society at large.
>
> (Martin and Osberg 2007, p. 39)

Zahra *et al.* (2009) argue that three types of social entrepreneurs can be iden-tified. The first type are social bricoleurs. These entrepreneurs are the ones who engage in addressing needs at a local level. The problems that they discover and deal with are often small-scale. The second type are social constructionists, who work on innovations at an institutional level, filling the gaps between existing services and tackling issues and needs that operating providers have not yet acknowledged. Finally, social engineers work on systemic change within larger structures. These entrepreneurs often replace old systems with new ways of doing things. Social engineers are thus engaged in more radical innovations than the other two types. Zahra *et al.* (2009) argue that there are key differences between the three types in "how they discover social opportunities (i.e. search processes), determine their impact on the broader social system, and assemble the resources needed to pursue these opportunities" (p. 520).

At the micro level, the social bricoleur might be the most common type of entrepreneur. However, on the other hand, there are many examples of social constructionists who listen to the voices of service users and use this information to shape new services that the social system does not provide. The interaction between the different levels is therefore of great interest, especially between initiatives at the micro level and how these can affect institutional structures and even change the socio-political discourse on social problems. It is important to analyse the relationship between citizens and different welfare institutions and how these institutions can become more emancipatory. Empowerment and participation does not come easy.

According to Svensson and Bengtsson (2010), social entrepreneurs only commercialize those innovations that are within their competence. If social entrepreneurs can get access to previous experience and knowledge, it makes it possible for them to identify new areas and thereby assess the possibilities of investing in innovative solutions that really are beyond their own area of expertise. Access to the unique experience and knowledge of a service user or users is a precondition for social entrepreneurs to create more accurate innovations that can address actual everyday problems. This type of innovation is often called user-driven innovation (Juul Kristensen and Voxted 2009). From the above discussion, we can conclude that an individual conducts social entrepreneurship. A social entrepreneur need not be active in a social enterprise, but may try to implement his or her social vision in a range of types of organization. It is not certain that the work will pay off and it need not be personal financial gain that is the driving force for the entrepreneur. A person who identifies the need for a handyman in the home care service, for instance, and establishes his own firm for meeting this need, is a social entrepreneur. He meets a social need, and if he succeeds, he earns a reasonable income. However, we expect him to balance the social engagement with the business element; if his profit is very high, we will question his social motives.

To clarify the difference between the three concepts – social enterprises, social entrepreneurship and social innovation – we can use microfinance as an example. Muhammad Yunus founded Grameen Bank in Bangladesh. Yunus, along with Grameen Bank, came to be awarded the Nobel Peace Prize in 2006. Yunus created the bank as a means of lending money to poor women in Bangladesh. These women were seen as lacking credit by all other banks. The idea was to lend out small sums of money without security to poor women. Yunus (2010) writes: "Lending to women in the poor villages of Bangladesh, we realized, was a powerful way to combat poverty for the entire society" (p. x). The concept of these small loans, called microcredits, has now spread and been scaled up in many other countries around the world. A key difference between Grameen Bank and other banks is that the borrowers own it. The bank also creates, through manageable loans, the conditions for giving the women's children the opportunity to go to school.

Yunus can thus be seen as a social entrepreneur, Grameen Bank as a social enterprise and microfinance as a social innovation. Returning to our example from the street newspaper movement, *The Big Issue*'s actual sales concept can be seen as a social innovation, Gordon Roddick and John Bird are social entrepreneurs and *The Big Issue* as an organization is a social enterprise.

A few barriers

An obvious barrier to social innovation is the political unwillingness to help marginalized groups. It is rare that groups such as the homeless become a central election issue. They represent an excluded group who do not have a strong organization and thus often have a rather weak voice politically and in the mainstream media. Instead, there are a number of moral assumptions about the homeless – that they have themselves to blame and that society should not prioritize helping people who make bad choices in life. The concept of social innovation can be perceived as rather tricky in social science research. The lack of clarity and its ambiguous connection to neo-liberal strategies have made some researchers abandon the concept in preference for sociological concepts such as social change. There is, in other words, some resistance.

Moulaert *et al.* (2005) show that initiatives created and developed at the grassroots level are often more innovative. These innovations are often initiated to tackle the prevailing system. The dilemma with these bottom-up social innovation initiatives is that when they become institutionalized, the solutions are often co-opted into the existing systems. Social innovation is seen as an opportunity to solve social problems. The idea of social innovations and organizations connected to working with social innovations can be seen as a rationalized myth – rational assumptions that are taken for granted. Ambient pressure, in the form of (for example) the EU's clear emphasis on social innovation, makes organizations express and present themselves as organizations that work with social innovations (Greenwood *et al.* 2008, p. 8). When social innovations are institutionalized, the pressure from the environment makes organizations adapt, and they tend to mimic other organizations within the same field. As a result, new models are introduced and implemented whether they solve a problem or not. This also points to the transferability problem of a social innovation. For instance, it is not obvious that a social innovation that successfully tackled a social problem in Australia can be transferred to a Spanish context and have equal impact. The importance of context should not be underestimated, as was discussed in Chapter 2. Moulaert *et al.* (2005) also argue that social innovations as products rather than processes have come to dominate, since there is a great demand for new and improved welfare services and products that are either not on the market yet or are no longer provided (p. 1976).

The concept of social innovation is widely used in many different contexts, and it is written about extensively in handbooks and readers (see also www.socialinnovationeurope.eu). Nevertheless, Mumford (2002) argues that social innovation is an overlooked domain; it has not yet received the attention it perhaps deserves. Another argument for this may be that all innovations are necessarily social in a sense, when they are developed in a social context. An argument put forward by Mumford and Moertl (2003) is that it is difficult to study social innovations – especially trying to trace the origin of ideas and identify the factors and mechanisms necessary to enable the implementation of a social innovation (p. 261).

Some possibilities

According to Phills *et al.* (2008, p. 36), the catalyst that is required for social innovations to emerge is the free movement of money, values, ideas and roles. An important aspect of social innovation is its function to "push" new technological innovations. One example is automatic test scoring. Another is the construction of a hygienic and self-cleaning toilet that can be used almost everywhere. In other words, there is a very interesting relationship between social innovation and new technology (Mumford and Moertl 2003). It was also Schumpeter's view that social innovations are necessary to facilitate economic growth and technological innovations (Moulaert *et al.* 2005, p. 1974).

Incremental innovation has been promoted as a viable strategy for organizational change (Popper 1945; Lindblom 1979; Ettlie *et al.* 1984), although more radical innovations may be perceived as having greater impact (Hartley 2005). Lindblom (1979) argues that small changes are preferable in terms of handling complex social problems. The dilemma of radical innovations is that it is very difficult to assess in advance their impact. A gradual process of trial and error creates the conditions for a cumulative development in which the social innovation is constructed by using several other innovations. This is in line with Popper's argument for incremental innovations (see Chapter 2).

An important driver of social innovations is strong leadership. We can use the terms "public champions" or "institutional entrepreneurs". Innovations do not appear out of the blue, but rather through institutional entrepreneurs or public champions who seek to mitigate or tackle an existing problem. A leader's ability to persuade others of a new idea's merits is of great importance.

According to Mumford and Moertl (2003, p. 264), there are a few other social factors needed to facilitate the implementation of social innovations:

- the ability to link social innovation with other initiatives;
- the innovation is congruent with emerging social trends;
- the core concept is flexible and adaptable;
- new technologies.

We refer to Cohen and Levinthal's (1990) concept of "absorptive capacity" several times in the book; the ability to capture new ideas and suggestions for change is essential for innovation. A high absorptive capacity can be seen as an antidote to overly strong path dependence (see Chapter 7).

Conclusion

Social innovation is a diffuse concept and rarely defined in a specific way. It is understood as a broad definition of social change that meets problems that are characterized as being social in nature. Often the concept is used in terms of social entrepreneurship or as equivalent to corporate social responsibility. We have in this chapter particularly highlighted the street newspaper movement as an example of social innovation, in which *The Big Issue* is a social enterprise and the founders John Bird and Gordon Roddick are social entrepreneurs. What scope is there for social innovations to tackle such challenging problems as poverty and homelessness? For the founder and director of Grameen Bank, poverty is not something created by the poor but by the system and the institutions that we have built up. For others, poverty is seen as something for which individuals have themselves to blame. The engagement in social innovation is connected to political positions. Social innovations are linked to social problems. This raises questions such as: to whom is something a problem and for whom is a social innovation a solution? A normative definition is that social innovations should lead to improvements for society in general. This is a vague goal and it is difficult to decide whom we should include, and when the goals are achieved. A more modest aim would be to state that social innovations should improve the situation of vulnerable groups. This can be the litmus test for social innovations.

4   Innovation in public services

> the State can not only facilitate the knowledge economy, but actively create it with a bold vision and targeted investment.
>
> (Mazzucato 2013, p. 2)

Many welfare services are a public responsibility. Even if they not are conducted by public actors, it is a public responsibility to make sure that there are services to take care of the poor, the elderly, the disabled and other vulnerable groups. This chapter discusses similarities and differences between public and private services, and points out the special demands to be met by public authorities. Successful innovations in public sector services need to take into account the peculiarities of the sector. Innovation in the public sector is not a contradiction; on the contrary, much innovative activity takes place. Towards the end of the chapter, the interplay between private and public actors is discussed.

Private and public: where to draw the line?

With her statement above about the active role of the state, Mazzucato enters into a long-standing debate. For centuries, the difference between the private and public sectors has been much written about. What ought to be private or public is an ideological question. Liberals will argue for a small public sector and the freedom for individuals to dispose of their own resources. On the other side, socialists will argue for a large public sector whereby public authorities collect and redistribute resources, giving people more equal opportunities to have a decent life. Freedom from poverty has been a slogan here.

Rousseau (1972) considered whether we can talk about a "general will". In recent decades, Jürgen Habermas (1991) has argued for a public sphere that is interpreted as a "discursive space in which individuals and groups congregate to discuss matters of mutual interest, and where possible, to reach a common judgement" (Hauser 1998, p. 86). It is an idealized presupposition that these deliberations can take place independent of the existing power structures. In these dialogues, the "best argument" will win and a consensus can be reached. This is a quite different situation from the democratic procedures followed by elected political bodies, whereby the majority wins the votes.

On the other side, we find an extreme liberal, Robert Nozick, who argued in *Anarchy, State and Utopia* (1974) that what people earn in an honest way no one has the right to take away from them (in the form of taxes). Only a minimal state could be seen as legitimate; only a state "limited to the functions of protection against force, theft, fraud, enforcement of contracts, and so on, could be justified without violating people's rights" (p. ix).

In his famous book *A Theory of Justice* (1971), John Rawls tried to construct a vision of a society that would be best for everyone. His point of departure was what we would prefer if we did not know anything about our position in society and had to choose beyond a "veil of ignorance".

These examples are meant to illustrate some of the variety of positions on what the public sector should be responsible for. All participants in this discussion will have to take a political position, even if that position is not made explicit.

Ideological positions, realized through political power, have of course influenced the construction of our societies, and they are important in our present societies through the ongoing political battles about the organization and reorganization of services. However, if we go back in history, we find that pragmatic reasons have also been important for solving common problems. Going a long time back, we find that some tribes needed to collaborate for hunting or fishing, or to organize themselves together to resist attacks from neighbouring tribes. These reasons contributed to "public" solutions (Moore Jr. 1984). In many cases, physical coercion has forced people into communities that they did not want. Some public units are created or initiated from the bottom up, but many also from the top down, where the participants do not have the opportunity to choose or decide. Religion has been important in the establishment of many states, and in their division (such as for India and Pakistan). If religion is also important in the laws and rules for everyday life, the space left for individual choice is restricted, and the powers of religious leaders are strong. In most Western societies today, the choice of religion is seen as a private matter. However, religious beliefs nevertheless influence political decisions in different ways, such as in Catholic Ireland where many women have to go abroad for abortions. In some Muslim countries, such as Iran, religious leaders play an active role in regulating everyday life.

Another route into the discussion (or study) of differences between private and public is to observe what the actual differences are in the society in which we live, how public and private actors behave, and what people expect. This will be our position. We find that, in spite of political disagreements, there seems to be a general consensus about some services that should be public, and some that should be private.

In Western societies, the courts, the armed forces and the police are seen as public responsibilities. Services for the poor are also, as mentioned, a public responsibility, because they cannot be solved adequately by the market or by the third sector. The service providers can be private (such as the Salvation Army), but the responsibility has to be left to public authorities, as does the financing. All societies have to draw the line between deserving and undeserving poor, and only those we consider as deserving should be recipients of public support.

At the private end of the spectrum, we find services most of us think of as private businesses, such as retailers, hairdressers and travel agents.

Between the poles of the spectrum, we find fields in which both public and private actors operate, either because we find it reasonable, or because there is political disagreement about where the responsibility should lie. Housing can be both public and private; transport and nursing homes can be provided by both public and private actors, and the same for medical and dental services. There is a large grey area between the poles. Established interplay and collaboration between private and public sectors, where the sharing of duties and responsibilities differs from case to case, can also be seen as part of the grey area.

So far, we conclude that it does not seem useful to draw sharp borders between private and public services. If we use three dimensions in this discussion – responsibility (for a given service), financing and provision – we can make a table with nine different combinations. If we take home care as an example, the public authorities have to make sure that it is a service for the needy, and they have to finance it (through tax revenue, contributions from the recipients, etc.), but they may have a tender to decide who is going to provide the service. Many people will then say that the services are privatized. We can define "private" as a service that is not controlled by the public system. However, "private" here has several meanings; the service can be conducted by market actors, non-profit actors (such as churches or the Red Cross) or informal helpers (such as neighbours, family or friends). Also between these categories we will find hybrids, such as social entrepreneurs who fulfil a social role but are able to survive in the market (see Chapter 3).

We find both collaboration and competition between these private actors (market actors may outbid non-profit actors in care, for instance), and we may have "blended" services, provided by actors who are both idealistic and compete in the market. It has been common to use a model with three actor groups (see Figure 4.1).

The public sector, the market, civil society and governance

Many cases blur the circles. For instance, if we are elected onto a board at our children's school, then we are part of the public system. If we are then on the committee to organize the celebrations to mark the end of the school year and get support from some local firms, and in addition benefit from much voluntary work, then the activity can be placed within all three circles.

In an archetypal model of the market, the communication between buyers and sellers is supposed to be through supply and demand. This is a natural regulation. However, in many connections this communication is insufficient; the buyers need more information about the product, they need to build a relationship of trust with the provider, and they may ask for a tailored service not

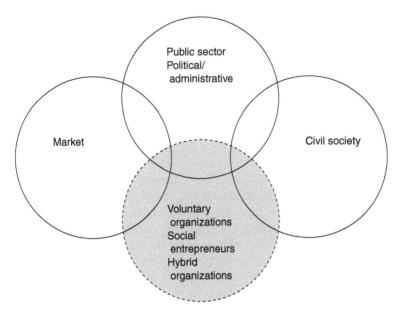

Figure 4.1 Actors in welfare services.

previously available in the market. This can be vital for an innovative development, and some economists have argued for an interactive market model (Lundvall 1988). However, it is still a crucial condition in the market that there is sufficient demand to make a profit from the offered service. If the market is not there in advance, it must be possible to create it.

When it comes to welfare services, the market cannot easily be a provider, because the recipients are often in need and lack the resources to handle their situation, and because it is needs rather than means that are the leading principle for the provision. In the market, the actors with the largest resources will be the winners, while in hospitals, most of us will agree that the patients with the greatest needs should have priority.

The establishment of welfare states in Europe can be seen as protection against the negative sides of the market. The welfare state was a de-commodification (Esping-Andersen 1990); workers did not have to sell their work (as a commodity) when they were unable to do a full man's job (because they were elderly, sick, disabled, etc.). Furthermore, a public distribution of goods should be a bulwark against the unfair distributions by the market. However, research has proven that resources are also important in the bureaucratic distribution of services. The system privileges people who can express themselves easily, and punishes the silent and uninformed, to use a saying from a Norwegian political scientist (Dahl Jacobsen 1967). We can see the system with a public distribution of resources as a three-step model. First, we have to prove that we are eligible to receive the service (we "really" are disabled); then, we have to wait in a line (where some have more priority than others); and finally, we come to the counter where we hopefully receive what we have asked for (Schaffer and Huang 1975).

Public services are established to meet people's needs and demands. However, expressed demands are always filtered through the understanding and priorities of the politicians in charge. This means that the politicians in charge can be seen as responsible for the failures of the system. A scarcity of public resources makes it necessary to prioritize between activities, and it is not easy for political committees. Politicians, in general, like to be identified with positive decisions and events, and not so much as those who refused cancer patients a new treatment because of the costs.

With the neo-liberal political winds of the late 1970s, the NPM recipe for more efficient service deliveries was to transfer responsibility for some services to market-based actors. Down-scaling the role of the public sector in service deliveries was seen as a vital innovative move (see Chapter 2). Some politicians would see such a move as a creative destruction (slimming the fat cat) and others as a destruction of important structures and competences. Now many seem to have recognized that the market-based model had limitations in the public sector, and for public services (Christensen and Lægreid 2002).

In her discussion of innovation in public services, Jean Hartley (2005) describes three paradigms, each of which "is a world view or a consistent pattern in that each contains particular conceptions and assumptions about the nature of the world, and the roles of the politicians, managers and the population" (p. 29). She labels them as "traditional" public administration, NPM and "networked governance" (NG). They can be linked to different ideologies and different historical periods, but they can also be seen as competing. Traditional public administration is the bureaucratic structure we knew from the pre-NPM period (and still find). NPM is already described, while NG is the model for the post-NPM period.

Innovations in the traditional model came in the form of some large-scale national and universal innovations; in NPM, we had innovations more in form than content; and in NG, we find innovations at both central and local levels, according to Hartley. In NG, the population can be seen as co-producers, while they were seen as customers in NPM and clients in the traditional model. Hartley's discussion pinpoints some important elements in dominant political thinking as well as in studies of public services. We can now find elements of all three paradigms side by side, but the focus on NG has been growing. Headings such as "from government to governance" (Kooiman 2003; Bovaird and Löffler 2003) are meant to encapsulate a development away from a traditional hierarchical model ruled by democratic political bodies at the top. In the government model, the public authorities are in control of the activities within their domains. By contrast, the governance model – also labelled as "new public governance" (NPG) (Osborne 2010) – can be seen more as a horizontal and fragmented system based on collaboration and partnership between public and private actors. The reason for developing such a fragmented model can be ideological; public authorities should share their duties and influence with private actors. However, it can also be pragmatic; in a complicated system with many actors operating together, no single actor has the power and resources to solve problems alone. Thus partnership and collaboration is the solution. The downscaling of the public sector, triggered by the ideology of NPM, has also contributed to a more fragmented and heterogeneous system that is more difficult for political authorities to manage (Peters 2010). In the governance model, it is vital that public–private partnerships improve quality for both service users and providers. Governance can then contribute to better goal attainment. However, collaboration and partnership will not always be a success. Internal competition, power struggles and conflicting goals may destroy projects and result in the rejection of desired improvements. It can also be complicated to lead a network in the desired direction, seen from the public authorities' perspective. There can be a need to impose some control over the components in governing, to find a form of meta-governance – a "governance of governance" (Peters 2010). The aim is to be "steering without rowing" (Osborne and Gaebler 1993). This has to be an indirect way of influencing the actors, different from the government model. The focus here has to be on results, ensuring they are in line with expressed goals (Moore and Hartley 2011). Management can be performed through regulating the frameworks (Veggeland 2009) or through different forms of management by objectives (MBO) (Drucker 1954).

There is a saying that what gets measured gets done. The corollary of this is that what cannot be easily measured runs the risk of not being done. There is a need to quantify and monitor goal attainment in this model, leaving out goals that are difficult to operationalize.

This is a book mainly for people working within social welfare and human services. The lessons from this section are that there are ongoing organizational innovations within the public sector, involving collaboration with private actors. It may be complicated to manoeuvre, and to understand the mechanisms, in the field. However, it is necessary to have an understanding of the dynamics, if people want to contribute to innovation within the field. In this interplay between private and public actors, it is also necessary to understand the core elements and values of the public sector. This will be the subject of the next section.

The peculiarities of the public sector

Public sector services have to follow established and accepted criteria for distribution

In a private company, it is considered not only acceptable but even positive to do a person or another company a favour and get a favour back in return, if it is to the benefit of the company. Within the public sector, these types of informal exchange will often be seen as corruption and cronyism. A manager in a public company is not allowed to sell a public building cheaply to a friend. Decisions have to be made according to rules for equal treatment and equal opportunities.

Around the year 2000 and the Millennium celebrations, British Prime Minister Tony Blair was criticized in the press for giving two Indian millionaires UK passports because they contributed a huge amount to the financing of the Millennium Dome, seen as Blair's project. If this had been true, it would have been a good bargain, since the costs of issuing passports are low compared to what the public sector received in return. The millionaires would probably not be a burden for the social welfare services in the future either. This example illustrates how prevalent an awareness of the rules we expect the public sector to follow is. The public sector has to abide by rules and procedures known in advance, established to ensure that all citizens are treated justly and fairly. Shortcuts taken with the aim of making services more efficient are not easily accepted.

In the justice system, people accused of crimes have the right to be defended, all arguments in favour of the accused should be brought forward and any doubt should be in favour of the accused. The procedures here are not very efficient, and are not meant to be. In Norway in 2011, one person (Anders Behring Breivik) was charged with killing 77 people, and he was obvious guilty. In spite of this, his trial was a very costly one. Trials, such as this one, are said to be important for confirming that a country is ruled by law. The reason for this is found in the constitutions of many countries, where it is stated that the society is built on some founding values, often specified in the legal texts. Improvements that make procedures more efficient may not be appreciated in this area.

The operation of the justice system is visible and important, but the rule of law has to be confirmed by thousands of decisions made in the public sector every day, such as granting planning permission to build a new house or accepting an application for a disability pension. These decisions are also ruled by laws and are subject to the same demands for fair treatment. To be efficient can then not be the primary goal, and transferring models directly from the private sector is therefore not possible. However, this is not the situation for all service deliveries. There are services, many within health and social care, that can in principle easily be provided by private actors. If we compare different countries here, we find solutions supplied by both private and public providers.

Goal attainment is prioritized over efficiency

A public service is established to realize a goal that political bodies, acting on behalf of the citizens, have decided is needed. This is the legitimacy of the service. A private company has to make profit over time, and if the activity is legal and the surplus reasonable, this will legitimate the activity. Profit is not a requirement for public services, despite the scarcity of public resources. However, public money must be spent in a responsible way, since it can always be used for other good purposes. If a branch of the public sector engages in the rehabilitation of people with reduced capacity in the labour market, bringing people back into work is the primary goal. Reducing costs by 50 per cent is not a measure of success if no one is brought back into the workforce. Reducing costs will always be a secondary (but important) aim.

Public services and public distribution are subject to democratic leadership

A consequence of the fact that profit is not a requirement for public bodies is that they do not need to be, or do not always need to be, demand-driven. They have to take into consideration objectives that are important for the society, and also adopt a longer-term planning strategy than the market. If all of the young people want to be fire fighters or hairdressers, for instance, the government has to make sure that the society educates doctors and engineers. Furthermore, political bodies can decide to support weak groups, while demands in the market can be dominated by strong groups with capital and other resources. Quotas for under-represented groups at universities can be seen as an effort to make good jobs available for formerly underprivileged groups. Although political leaders can ignore expressed demands from citizens, they need to get support and legitimacy in the long run, if they want to be re-elected.

The role of politicians in the public sector is in many ways to be innovators; they try to sell new solutions to public problems and aim to convince the majority that their solutions are the best. A revolution can be seen as the ultimate innovation; society should be organized in a totally new way. However, a revolution is difficult to sell to a majority. The choice of solutions more often takes place within established frameworks, but small steps can over time develop new models of society.

Public services are often more complex than private

In a very simplified view, a private business only needs to deliver services that enough customers buy to give the company a profit. By contrast, public sector departments need to realize many, and often partly conflicting, goals simultaneously. For instance, the traffic authorities have as a primary objective to make it possible to travel from A to B as fast as possible. However, they are also responsible for road safety, and are obliged to reduce pollution and work towards a cleaner environment.

In the field of welfare services, we know that a social service should both help the claimants and control them, a difficult combination at the counter. People come to a social service office because they are in need of help, and a primary task for the service is to help the needy, but it should also prevent fraud, ensure equal treatment and follow the rules. The staff at the counter have to control information and in some ways treat applicants as suspects. This duality is not easy to handle, and sometimes people get economic support but feel humiliated when they leave the office. It is easier for charitable organizations, who can distribute help without controlling the recipients. European studies show that people are more satisfied with help given by religious organizations than with help given by the public sector (Bäckstrøm *et al.* 2011). However, it has not yet been proven that this would still be the case if they had to control the recipients.

The political objectives for social services are extensive, and this complexity can sometimes result in an improvement in one field having unforeseen negative consequences in another (Considine *et al.* 2009). Inspired by models from private enterprises, there have been efforts to reorganize the public sector and split it up into smaller units. The goal is to try to get "unipurpose units", in which it would be easy to establish indicators of success. However, a critique of the public sector as it stands is that different parts do not seem to be co-ordinated; one branch is often in conflict with another. The ministry for the oil and gas sector, for instance, has a different purpose to the ministry for the environment. Problems with a lack of co-ordination will probably be greater if we split the public sector into smaller units.

Public services are quite different from private services, and sometimes it can be difficult to even see them as services. No one is happy to pay tax and then to receive services from the tax authorities. Being imprisoned and subject to these "services" is not appreciated by the "customers" who would rather remain at liberty. For these services, we can see society as a whole as the customer.

"Wicked problems" is a term used to point out the complexity in public problem-solving. The phrase was originally used in social planning to describe problems that are difficult or impossible to solve because of incomplete, contradictory or changing requirements that are often difficult to recognize. The term "wicked" is used to denote resistance to resolution rather than evil (Australian Public Service Commission 2007). Examples can be international drug trafficking, prostitution, crime and social injustice. Even if these problems are "wicked", the public sector needs to have programmes to mitigate or fight them, and the field is open for innovative solutions.

Risk-taking is limited in the public sector

For private firms, it is crucial not to invest more than they can afford and handle. If they do, they do not survive in the market. However, if the shareholders or the private owners take a risk and fail, they lose their own money. If a responsible person in a public body takes a risk on behalf of his organization and fails, it is not his own money. In Norway, some municipalities invested in high-risk financial products in the US, and in 2008 it was obvious that they had lost huge amounts of municipal money. It was a newsworthy story because they lost money, but in principle it would had been unacceptable even if they had made a profit. Municipal money belongs to the public, and should be invested in a transparent way and in line with established principles.

Iceland after the crisis of 2008 is an example of how private actors can put burdens on innocent people and the public sector. A few people within the leading banks had taken risks that the banks did not manage when the crisis came. Both the Icelandic state and innocent people in many countries (not least in the UK) got into financial trouble. A lesson from these cases is that private actors also have to limit their gambling to what they themselves can be responsible for.

These are extreme examples, and concern economic investment. However, there are other forms of risk-taking that also have to take place within given frameworks but that should be promoted. One is the risk-taking involved in finding new and innovative ways of solving wicked and existing problems. In the private sector, the majority of innovations are failures, but still the imperative to innovate remains. The bonus in private business is the profit from being first on the market with new and desirable products. There is no such bonus for being a pioneer in the public sector, but there is still a need to pay the costs of investment in failures in terms of both time and money. A carrot in the public sector is the satisfaction of doing things better for service users and employees, and in many cases saving resources. If we want to promote innovation in the public sector, it has to be accepted that there will be both successes and failures. We cannot stimulate creativity and a search for new solutions without a culture that accepts failures (see Chapter 8).

One way of reducing the risk of innovations failing is to see what happens and works for similar organizations. Municipalities will adopt successes from other municipalities, and states can learn from other states.

What is the value of public innovations?

It we accept that profit, or added economic value, is not the only relevant goal for public innovations, what should it be, then? With his book *Creating Public Value: Strategic Management in Government* (1995), Mark Moore started a large and important debate about what "public value" is. We have already commented on the debate about the term "public", so the concern now is with the term "value". It is not a very precise term, and we could say with Van Wart (1966) that "values is a relative term based on relative preferences" (p. 458). Moore argued that the task of public leaders is to create value in the same way as private actors: "creating results that are valued and showing that ... the resources spent to achieve those results could not be better spent on other activities, for instance private consumption" (1995, p. 29). This is an economic definition similar to those used in micro-economics, and the goal is added economic value. Others in the same tradition have stated that added value will either be an improved product or an improved efficiency (Cole and Barston 2006). The legacy from private business is clear. The importance of quality is not clearly included in these definitions. Critics found the concept too narrowly defined, and mentioned values embedded in the public sector ethos that we have commented on below. In response, Moore has since given a much broader definition (Benington and Moore 2011) in which social, political, cultural and environmental dimensions are added to the concept of public value. Bason (2010) has added service experience and democracy as values in public innovation. This brings us in line with the conclusion of an earlier section – that the public sector should handle wicked problems and realize many (and conflicting) goals simultaneously.

Public activity and innovations will be evaluated according to two sets of values. The first are what we could call "input values", based on fundamental values from the constitution (justice, equal treatment of equal cases, and so on). Beck-Jørgensen and Bozeman (2007) analysed academic literature about the public sector and found a large set of values that the authors expected to find in the public sector. In a comparative study of values in public administration in 28 EU states and applicants in 2006, many of the same values were expressed. "Rule by law", "duty of care" and responsibility were three of the most frequently mentioned (Moilanen and Salminen 2007). These input values are frameworks for public activity. However, we also expect results ("output values"), as stressed in Moore's first book. Then the question is what the result of an innovative activity should be. We need to have a qualified answer to that before we start.

Public activity and innovations have to navigate between both the input and the output values. Some of the input values, grounded in the constitution, will always have to be taken into account. The prioritizing of output values needs to be discussed in each individual case. However, a modest conclusion for social welfare and human services is that innovations that carry added social and/or health values can be important for public services, even if they bring higher costs in the short term. A breakthrough in some fields of cancer treatment will definitely add public value.

Who are the public champions?

We have already mentioned the Beacon Scheme, the UK's national award programme to encourage innovation and excellence in local government (see Chapter 2). The programme aims both to reward excellence and to disseminate good ideas and models (Hartley 2008). In the US, the Innovation in American Government Program was set up in 1986. Since the programme was launched, 400 outstanding government innovations have been recognized (Rizvi 2008). Studies of the US programme challenge the stereotype of the risk-averse bureaucrat who is awaiting orders from his or her political masters. Instead they find public servants who try to determine public expectations and needs, and undertake initiatives to meet them. They also find that innovations can be seen as an equal-opportunity phenomenon that can be initiated at all levels of government, from elected politicians to front-line workers (Borins 2008). Bottom-up innovations occur much more frequently than conventional wisdom would indicate, and middle-managers are much more active in initiating innovations than executives (Borins 2001). The conclusion is that public entrepreneurs, or public champions, can be found at all levels of public administration. This is an argument for employee-driven innovation (EDI), and will be discussed further in Chapter 8.

The public sector as an engine for private innovations

So far, we have been concerned with innovative activity within the public sector. It is important for the citizen that the public sector adapts to the opportunities presented by innovations in the private sector, and it is important for the private sector that the public sector is an up-to-date and competent partner, so that the private sector gets the assistance it needs. The public sector is important for businesses in the private sector in many ways, such as regulating the markets, improving transport and ensuring energy supply.

The public sector can be an innovator in its own right, but has also played a significant role for innovation in the private sector. The public sector has been responsible for the development of many of the technologies that surround us today (Windrum 2008). The internet and the World Wide Web were developed by public bodies, as were many other innovations with which private enterprises can now make huge profits. According to some studies, the state is still entrepreneurial (Mazzucato 2013).

The public sector is vital to private innovation in educating competent people, and in performing research that is important for private businesses. The state is important for providing infrastructure and logistics, in building roads and producing energy, for instance. The public sector also has programmes for assisting private businesses in innovative activities. The scope of these programmes will vary from country to country, depending of the understanding of the role of the state in that specific political system.

5 Public innovation

A question of power?

In this chapter, we look at innovations as a part of the permanent ongoing struggle for power and influence in society. Terms such as "drivers" and "barriers" are often used in case studies for an understanding of innovation processes. We try to show that these can be applicable concepts, but that innovations can also be seen as a result of power relations and constellations. Innovation is a question of power, and it is a fight for defining both the problem and the solution.

Introduction

Bismarck's comment in the epigraph above pinpoints the fact that strength and competence determines what can be realized in politics. The public sector is ruled by democratically elected bodies at all levels (municipalities, counties, states), so from a formal point of view it is easy to point out the decisive power. Politicians have the power to conduct innovations. Political innovations are common and they can be radical. The only formal restriction for radical innovations is the constitution, and the constitution can also be changed.

It is easy to find examples of wide-ranging public innovations. The establishment of the NHS in the UK has already been mentioned (see Chapter 2). Over time, we can see that the public sector has expanded into new fields and established new public committees or ministries. The acknowledgement of new problems, such as global warming and pollution, contributed to the establishment of ministries for the environment in many countries. The ministries represent different values, and even if they all belong to the public sector and are ruled by the same government, they may have quite conflicting positions.

In Norway, the organization of ownership and production of oil from the North Sea can be seen as a successful innovation. When oil resources were discovered, strong forces pushed for the adoption of the same models that had been used in many countries before, leaving the production to big companies that should bear the cost and take a reasonable profit, paying tax to the state.

However, some public entrepreneurs within the dominant party (the Social Democrats) had both the vision and sufficient power to set up a public company for both the production and the administration of the resources. This model earned huge public incomes, and a public fund was established. In December 2013, the fund passed 5,000bn kroner (more than 600bn euro), leaving each citizen with more than 120,000 euro if the fund was to be shared equally. In addition, the organization of oil production gave birth to a national industry competent in deep-sea drilling. This success makes it difficult to reject radical public innovations in Norway.

Power and politics

Politics has been seen as the "authoritative allocation of values" (Easton 1953, p. 129). Authority is the right of a person or institution to make decisions affecting the community (Kingdom 1999). We see these decisions as legitimate because they are made according to rules and laws that we accept. Political committees are established to handle decision-making in situations in which citizens have conflicting interests. Normally power here is connected to having the majority on the committee. The definition above can be extended in two ways. First, values can be supplemented with goods. Many employees want higher salaries to be able to buy more goods, while the employers want to keep them down, because they are sharing the same surplus, and in some ways the same value. In the sharing of money and other goods, compromises can be made. Our second extension is to point out that the conflicts about how to share arise because the resources are scarce. No one can get all they want.

If two parties are in conflict about the interpretation of a religion, compromises are more difficult. Innovations in the public sector will influence both the distribution of goods and the balance between values.

It is important to keep in mind that political decisions are not only made by political committees. If General Motors decides to shut down a car factory in a small town, the decision obviously influences the allocation of goods and values in that community, even more than decisions at the local political level often do. However, the decision is made by the firm. The mass media execute political power through the stories they focus on and the way they report them; interest groups and smaller groups are also actors in the political arena; and bureaucrats, who according to Weber's (1964) definition are neutral, nevertheless make decisions with political implications.

A classic definition of power was given by Robert Dahl in 1957: A has power over B if A can get B to do something that B would not otherwise do (Lukes 2005). This is an actor-oriented definition, and the power base can be money, physical power, etc. However, the actors do not work in a vacuum. Power is also embedded in structures and rules in society, in favour of some competences and capacities. Money is a useful source of power and influence in many markets, but is not seen as a valid source of power in politics. However, we know, not least from the US, that money is needed for political campaigns, limiting the number of available candidates for important positions. The book title *The Best Democracy Money Can Buy* (Palast 2002) underlined this situation.

Discursive theory has drawn attention to power exercised through language and the way in which we describe a phenomenon. Often one explanation attains a hegemonic status, becoming the dominant understanding of the phenomenon in society (for instance, "Jobless people are lazy and do not want to work"). If we want to study how innovations are dependent on the actors' power, it is tempting (and relevant) to focus on decisions. However, we must also bear in mind that power can be executed in these other mentioned forms, and as non-decisions. When we go to work on a day when we "really" are sick, for instance, it is not necessarily because our boss has told us to do it. It may also be because we anticipate that they, or our colleagues, will appreciate it.

The main reason for mentioning these elementary definitions in our context is that innovations in the public sector must be seen as a part of the struggle between different interests in society. There is a conflict of interests whenever we have decision situations with more than one possible outcome. We can ask for whom the innovation is an improvement (see Chapter 2).

Employees in public administration are today no longer only rule-oriented bureaucrats; they are also professionals with a strong loyalty to their profession (such as engineers, medical doctors and social workers). At the same time, professionals in welfare services are concerned with taking care of the interests of users, and this can be a challenging balance to strike in innovative work in the field. An improvement for the professionals may not be an improvement for the service users. The workload in welfare services is often very high, and it is tempting to push more tasks over to service users.

A top bureaucrat in a Danish municipality sees this as an important route to innovation in welfare services: "the individual citizen [will] herself take a larger responsibility for her own and her relatives' welfare" (Zealand Care 2014, our translation). This can obviously be seen as an effort to roll back the welfare state and reduce public services.

For professionals who claim to be user-oriented, it must be a necessary exercise to work out the consequences of innovations for service users, and especially for the most vulnerable groups. How to empower vulnerable groups is a major debate in the field, but some groups will be in need of advocates outside their own group. These discussions are very familiar to people working in the field, together with the two sets of values ("input" and "output") mentioned in Chapter 4. Working in the public sector involves the art of balancing values and demands that can often seem to be in conflict. Innovative work is no exception here. However, since this is the complex reality, there are no easy shortcuts or ways around. Innovations conducted by people in the field need to take this reality into account. A condition then is that people in the field see the possibilities for changes and innovations. The final responsibility for innovations and changes lies with political committees.

In the literature about innovation, we find few studies that explicitly discuss power and power relations between actors. One explanation for this might be that economists have been the dominant authors of this literature (Fagerberg and Verspagen 2009). For economists, power structures are embedded in the market and our relative power is connected to our position either on the demand side or the supply side. An important exception to the dominant economic perspective is one of the best-known books about innovation, namely Everett Rogers' book *Diffusion of Innovations* (2003). Rogers' approach is sociological and he focuses on the actors' interests and needs.

In his discussion of what makes the diffusion of innovations successful, Rogers underlines the diversity of innovations. It took only few years before mobile phones were widely used by a large number of people (a consumer innovation), while it can take decades to change behaviour (such as the use of seat belts in the US). Rogers defines diffusion as the process by which an innovation is disseminated through defined channels over time among members of a social system. In explaining the differences in the speed of diffusion, he refers to five properties of innovations (discussed below). These are useful for understanding why some innovations are successful and widely diffused, while others are not.

We can talk about different phases through which an innovation must pass. The process starts with a new invention or a new idea; next, a decision has to be made about initiating an innovation; and finally, the innovation has to be disseminated to the groups or areas for whom it was meant.

Let us use medical support for drug addicts as an example. The inventions are new medications that can help them to handle their addiction, such as subutex (buprenorphine). Once a medication has been tested, the political authorities have to decide whether it can be used in the treatment of defined groups. Then the information about what it is and how it can be used has to be disseminated. The target group is not easy to reach, they may be sceptical about co-operating with the welfare services, and they may be an unstable group to treat.

When politicians make a decision, it does not necessarily mean that it will be implemented. Some decisions are intended to be symbolic (Edelman 1985), and in other situations politicians make decisions in principle but do not allocate sufficient resources to realize the goals. Innovations need both resources and actors who are dedicated to implementing them. An innovation will often have to challenge established structures and understandings, and will therefore often be more demanding to realize than changes that fit into such structures and understandings.

Without implementation, we have no innovation. Innovations can turn out to be different from the original idea when they are implemented. Such adaptations (or new innovations) can be the result of a compromise between the actors, of power and bargaining processes, or of learning and new insights gained during the implementation process.

Rogers' model of diffusion

Rogers does not explicitly explain the diffusion of an innovation with respect to the interests of the actors. However, his model can be used as a point of departure. He focuses on five different characteristics of innovation (Rogers 2003).[1]

Relative advantage

"Relative advantage" refers to "the degree to which an innovation is perceived as being better than the idea it supersedes" (Rogers 2003, p. 15). It can be measured in different ways, depending on what is most important for the perceiver: social prestige, economy, working conditions, etc. What matters is whether the innovation is perceived as advantageous. Moreover, the greater the expected advantage is, the more rapid the rate of adoption will be, according to Rogers. We will qualify that statement and put it like this. Public innovations will have consequences for different groups. The larger the expected advantage is for a group, the more interested it will be in realizing the innovation. And the other way around – the less advantageous the innovation is perceived to be, the less interested the group will be in its realization. If a group feels it is threatened by the realization of an innovation, it can actively work against it. If an innovation is expected to be to the benefit of one group but to the detriment of another, we cannot expect the support of the latter.

The reasoning above is based on the assumption that the actors are informed and able to act rationally. That may not be true. Vulnerable groups do not easily get information about the consequences of decisions, and they are often unable to organize and promote their own interests. In a system in which access to relevant information is important, they can be losers. The distribution of services within a public system does not follow the logic of the market, but resources are still needed in many contexts.

Compatibility

"Compatibility" refers to "the degree to which an innovation is perceived as being consistent with the existing values, past experiences, and needs of potential adopters" (Rogers 2003, p. 15). An idea that is incompatible with existing values and norms will be adopted more slowly than one that is not. An idea that is incompatible often requires the prior adoption of a new set of values.

These statements can be interpreted in different ways. One is to say that the less radical an innovation is, the easier it will be to get it accepted. Here it is also important to mention that an innovation will affect different groups. The recipients are seldom one unified group with a common interest. Compatible new solutions are easy to understand. However, if there is an acceptance within an organization that things have to be done quite differently for it to survive, a compatible solution may be seen as less favourable than a completely new one.

Complexity

"Complexity" is "the degree to which an innovation is perceived as relatively difficult to understand and use" (Rogers 2003, p. 16). New ideas that are easy to understand and implement are adopted more quickly than more complicated ones. This seems to be obvious. In implementing innovations, however, there can be a tendency to overestimate the recipients' ability to receive and digest information. Public services put much of their information on the internet, and expect that people have access to PCs and understand the given instructions. However, there are many cases that prove that people do not understand how to fill out electronic forms and that the service user interface expects too much. People working in service design argue for more visual instruction and less text (Polaine *et al.* 2013).

Trialability

"Trialability" is "the degree to which an innovation may be experimented with on a limited basis" (Rogers 2003, p. 16). New ideas that can be tried out in installments will generally be adopted more quickly than those innovations that cannot be split up.

Public authorities have been criticized for starting too many test projects instead of establishing a permanent model. However, small-scale projects can be very useful as a way of learning and correcting mistakes before going full-scale. This is in line with Popper's recommendation for an incremental strategy (see Chapter 2).

Observability

"Observability" is "the degree to which the results of an innovation are visible to others" (Rogers 2003, p. 16). The easier it is for individuals to see the results of an innovation, the more likely they are to adopt it. The same is true for the decision-makers; if a project can give observable results, it is easier to convince others to participate and to reorganize their activities accordingly.

In spite of the usefulness of Rogers' model as a way into the study of power and conflicts, his model has been criticized for being too harmonic, and for ignoring the power of the actors and their possible active resistance. "Diffusion" is often used as a term in chemistry, describing a process in which liquids or gases pass through obstacles, or intermingle with other liquids, gases or solids. Transferred to the field of innovation, the term implies that it is only a matter of time before innovations spread. However, like democracy in an authoritarian regime, it is not inevitable that they will be implemented.

Based on empirical studies, Rogers has categorized adopters of innovations by how quickly they take up new innovations. He finds a bell curve here; there are a few innovators, then a larger number of early adopters, then the early and late majority, and finally the laggards. According to Rogers, we can find this distribution for the spread of all innovations. It is an intuitive model; we know from our neighbourhood some people who took up the latest technological innovation early, and we also know some laggards who insisted on continuing to use a typewriter instead of a laptop. Often it seems to be the same people who are first every time, but there may also be discrepancies; for instance, some hospitals have very new and advanced technologies for screening and testing, but at the same time resist the use of electronic journals.

Drivers of innovation: the example of the pharmaceutical industry

Many case studies include a discussion of drivers and barriers, but these are not necessarily only actors. Laws and rules, and cultural and structural conditions, can also be seen as both drivers and barriers.

New technological opportunities are obviously important drivers of innovations in many fields, and are innovations in themselves. In health services, they can cure and treat more than ever, and the expectations of what can be repaired are rising. However, technological developments also trigger new solutions in elderly care.

In welfare services, the medical industry, and especially pharmaceutical firms, are important drivers of innovations. The role of these firms will be discussed in more detail, to illustrate that different actors can have both common and divergent interests. Our position is that it is often useful to focus on the actors and their legitimate interests to gain a better understanding of the destiny of a proposed innovation.

Within the large firms in the pharmaceutical industry, huge sums of money are spent on research. New inventions are transformed into innovations in collaboration with medical doctors in the field. Marketing to doctors is allowed, speeding up the diffusion process. New medicines and drugs have helped large numbers of patients to enjoy a better and longer life. However, there are still many challenges; there are unsolved problems for the treatment of cancer, dementia and other diseases. We are still waiting for the final breakthrough. The new drugs have helped people and also earned the firms great profits. They are obviously important drivers in their struggle for curing diseases and for increasing their own profits.

"Medicalization" has been defined as a process whereby an increasing number of problems in everyday life are explained using a medical model and treated with medical instruments (Zola 1972). Pharmaceutical firms contribute to both curing existing diseases and "inventing" new ones. The *Diagnostic and Statistical Manual of Mental Disorders* (DSM), used for the categorization of diseases in the US, contained 106 diagnoses in 1952 and almost 300 in 1994 (Mayes and Horwitz 2005). For psychosomatic illnesses and especially for mental illnesses, it can be debated how deviant we can be without being diagnosed. If the accepted tolerance level for high blood pressure is set to a lower level, more people will be prescribed medication. High blood pressure is not a disease; it is a symptom, but is often treated as a disease. An important growing trend has been "off-label" use. This is when a drug is used in fields other than those for which it was developed. These extended applications are very profitable for the firms. For instance, a medicine (Paxil) was developed for the depression market but it was also advertised as a cure for "social phobia", which was defined as "fear of social and performance situations in which embarrassment may occur" (Conrad 2007, p. 17). The sale of antidepressants in Sweden is now seven times higher than it was in 1993, without any documented rise in mental problems that can explain the increased consumption. More than 6 per cent of the population is either using or has access to these drugs daily (SOU 2009:89 2009). A Swedish study found that three out of four residents in a nursing home lacked a diagnosis that would justify the fact that they were being treated with antidepressants (Ulfvarsson 2004). Overmedicalization may be profitable for firms but have problematic side-effects for service users.

An innovation, and an alternative to medication, in the treatment of dementia is the use of music. The therapeutic use of music is said to have reduced the need for drugs for many patients. In the UK, organizations such as Singing for the Brain, Music for Life, Lost Chord and Golden Oldies "have made it possible for every care home in the country to have access to live musicians, both professional and amateur, most of them trained to deal with the special needs of an elderly, memory-impaired audience" (Age UK n.d.). The same approach is also used in other countries. Workers in welfare services will sometimes be at a crossroads where they have to choose between different directions for an innovation, and where each direction has its own convincing proponents.

The conclusion of this section is that a central group of actors, responsible for many innovations in social and health care, are drivers of innovations, but are also driven by their own interests. These interests may not always be the same as the interests of staff or service users. An analysis of their power is important for an understanding of their innovative role and the side-effects of their proposals. Innovations are part of the power-play in society.

Innovations in elderly care: some possible scenarios[2]

Since the capacity of the elderly care system is worrying politicians in many countries, possible scenarios for elderly care can be used as further illustration that innovations can take different directions into the future, and that each direction will have different supporters. Combinations can be possible, but at some crossroads we will have to choose which one direction to take. The focus of the scenarios is not primarily on the costs, but on how the need for "helping hands" can be met. From the public debate, we can construct five models, which are described in simplified terms below.

Improved salaries, working conditions and workloads

This scenario presupposes that the government declares care to be a central responsibility of the public sector, and that this must imply that the salaries for carers (nurses, home helpers, etc.) must be increased relative to comparable groups, and the working conditions and workloads must also be improved. Together, these changes should make work in the care sector more attractive compared to other sectors. The care sector can then attract a larger share of the workforce and recruit more young people.

Drivers here will be the employees and their unions, and the politicians supporting the unions. Counter-forces will be other unions (such as teachers' unions) whose members do not accept being left behind. It is also a costly innovation, since care workers are a large group in society.

Imported care

Unemployment and low salaries in the Baltic states, the Balkans and the new EU members from Eastern Europe open the way for the import of both carers and professionals from these countries. This model works partly as an innovation already, with private firms importing workers from the East. However, the main import so far has been male workers for construction work. To solve the care deficit in the (relatively) more developed countries, the import of workers needs to be much better organized and on a larger scale. Some politicians will be afraid of care worker immigration, because some carers will stay permanently, such as nurses finding local husbands. Other politicians will see this as a desirable situation. On a large scale, the import solution will result in a care deficit in the exporting countries, and perhaps also in a drain of professionals (doctors and nurses), which can be seen as unethical.

Drivers in this scenario will be importing companies and employers in need of care workers (both public and private). Counter-forces will be labour unions and professional organizations, who will see the import of workers as a threat to their wages and bargaining position.

Technological solutions

When a staff shortage is the starting point, it is reasonable to try to find solutions that reduce the need for more staff, and ways of using the staff already employed more efficiently. Sickness absence is high in many areas of the care sector, and one reason for this is that care work is physically demanding. The installation of lifters is a good preventive measure, but there are lots of other options here: communication technology with screens, microchips for people with dementia so they can be traced if they go missing, "intelligent homes", etc. Technological innovations are regularly introduced, but if the real usage is compared to what is possible, most countries have a technological deficit. The effective use of technology demands an organization in which it is integrated in a robust model, and in which it is easy to educate service users and get support for technological problems.

Drivers of innovations here will be firms delivering technological solutions, and technologically minded people. Counter-forces could be professional organizations resisting a "robotization" of care, and also organizations representing service users who might resist what they see as a "dehumanization" of care.

Increased use of volunteers

Volunteering can take different forms. Relatives, friends and neighbours do a great job of providing informal care, reducing the need for public care. If one woman takes care of her husband with dementia on a full-time basis, this is equivalent to the work of 2.5 helpers (estimate from Norway) in an institution. This type of care has the quality of being tailored to the individual, because giver and receiver know each other and have an emotional relation. This is often both love and labour.

Volunteering can be organized through non-profit organizations, such as the Red Cross and Salvation Army. In these organizations, people are treated as part-time employees; they have contracts and they are trained for "the job".

In some countries, we now also find centres that organize volunteer activities, where people can just turn up and where they do not need to commit themselves for a longer period. Some of the activities in these centres are for the volunteers themselves (dancing, playing cards, etc.) and some are organized activities for helping vulnerable groups with care. The centres can be organized by groups of organizations, or as public–private partnerships.

The amount of voluntary work done in the care system is equivalent to a huge number of employees, so if all volunteering stopped, the public care system would break down in most countries.

In Nordic countries, there is a declared desire to increase the use of volunteers in home care (see, for instance, NOU 2011:11 2011), but the recipe for this is still vague. An important question concerns the resources: are there sufficiently large unused resources for this purpose in society? If the answer is positive, the next question is how to transfer the resources into the care system. Here there is scope for innovations. New forms of public–private partnership may be necessary.

Drivers in this scenario will be groups of relatives, voluntary organizations and politicians who support a smaller public sector. Counter-forces will be professional organizations, since the scenario could imply that some of the tasks conducted by employees today will be given to voluntary "amateurs".

Mandatory care

Innovations in the four directions mentioned so far can reduce but not solve the lack of helping hands; they can all be seen as incremental innovations. A radical innovation called "solidarity care" has been proposed in Norway, in a Green Paper (NOU 2011:11 2011). The background is that compulsory military service has now been scrapped in many countries, but in some countries young people can be still called up for a year. The rest of the cohort could then spend a year in the care system, get some elementary education and work under supervision. This would result in a significant increase in the number of helping hands. It can be seen as reasonable that everyone should have to devote a year to society, and this scenario could result in a better understanding between generations.

Some people see it as the opposite of volunteering; this is forced care, conducted by unqualified staff. A model for a care system that meets these objections could be organized, but we have not yet seen a serious proposal for such a model.

Drivers here will be some relatives and some politicians who have realized that there is a shortage of staff in the sector today. This group does not see any other way out of the crisis. However, there will also be some resistance from other relatives, and strong resistance from professional organizations in favour of the first scenario.

Some of the scenarios can co-exist better than others. Higher salaries and more technology can go well together, but there may be conflicts where nurses want more staff but not more technology. However, higher salaries and a higher status for care workers do not go well together with the other three scenarios. At the municipal level, and at other levels of public administration, many decisions are made that aim to innovate and improve the care system. There we can study how the actors argue for their preferred scenarios for the future of the care system. Perhaps we will find further scenarios not mentioned above.

Conclusion

Innovation is taught using case studies. One of the authors conducted a case study on the diffusion of learning and coping centres in Norway (Rønning 2014). One conclusion from that study is that within health services, medical doctors have a decisive power. The whole system is built on their competence, and if they do not co-operate it is difficult to make progress. Innovations have to be licensed by doctors. To put it in Rogers' terms, they have to be seen as relative advantages by doctors, and to be compatible with their perspectives. Monopoly power is a challenge for innovations. However, an understanding of the power structure in the field in which we work is a prerequisite for a successful innovation. We need to be creative and have new and good ideas, but their successful implementation in the public sphere depends on how well we can understand, communicate with and bargain with other actors in the field. Political craftsmanship is needed.

Notes

1 Parts of the text in this section are taken from Rønning (2014).
2 These scenarios were introduced in Rønning (2009).

6 Levels of innovation

People don't resist change. They resist being changed.

(Senge 1990, p. 155)

From many sources, we know that services that should be developed *for* users have to be developed *with* users. In this chapter, we will discuss how this can be done at different levels, but with a specific focus on micro-level innovation. There are many examples of innovations at a micro level including self-building projects, the creation of low-carbon communities and self-help groups such as Alcoholics Anonymous (AA). We will also discuss the implications of user-driven innovations for developing inclusive practices within the welfare sector. By viewing service users' own experiences as an important source of knowledge, co-creative initiatives can take place.

There is a significant difference between user-led innovations within social welfare and human services and those in product development in the technological field. User-driven innovation in the technological field has often tried to identify lead users who have the capacity to enhance a product or envision new types of products. Many service users have experience of being marginalized; their voices are not often heard. Finding ways to make use of service users' own experiences is therefore related to other kinds of challenges in order to create real influence and participation.

Introduction

People resist being changed because they want to be involved in decisions affecting the services they use. Over the past decade, service user influence and service user involvement have attracted greater interest within the human service sector. There are several reasons why service users are central in changing existing practices or developing new solutions in social services. Two parallel processes have driven the renewed interest in service user participation. One is the consumerist approach, which is a market-led approach in which the consumer is seen as king. The other is a democratic approach based on empowerment, social justice and social inclusion (Beresford 2002; Denvall *et al.* 2007). The strongest movement has probably been the disabled people's movement. A famous phrase from this movement is "Nothing about us, without us", which relates to the epigraph above that states that people do not mind change as long as they are not forced to change. This transformative function is one of the key ingredients in human service organizations and therefore also the key challenge for service user involvement in human services. These movements and service user organizations have fought not only for social justice and human and civil rights, but also for involvement in the development of services that they use. One good example of a service that empowers service users is user-led personal assistance. Services tend to work poorly if their users are not involved. Service users' own experiences are of great importance for developing innovations within welfare services.

Different forms of participatory methods have been created in order to engage and empower communities and neighbourhoods in social change work. Another trend is the use of art and design to create platforms for change. There has been an increase in the creation of living labs and design labs (Almirall and Wareham 2008; Björgvinsson *et al.* 2010).

There are, however, many complicating barriers that hinder the participation of users in the development of innovative services and products. One barrier is the question of knowledge and expertise. Another is the question of choice. Many service users who have to use public services lack the resources to be able to influence the services provided. Service users do, however, have great knowledge of their own situation. It is this knowledge and experience that could enhance the services that are being developed.

Innovations at different levels

Micro-level innovations differ from innovations at the meso and macro levels. However, there are many examples of innovations that affect all levels. Innovations at the macro level concern structural changes and society's capacity to fuel innovations (Mazzucato 2013). The creation of the welfare state or the introduction of general pension insurance could be seen as examples of macro-level innovations. With hindsight, the welfare state seems to be a radical innovation; compared to a liberal state with limited responsibility, the welfare state takes a much more active responsibility for the well-being of citizens, and also for the redistribution of wealth. The Nordic countries' welfare states were the most far-reaching (Esping-Andersen 1990), but many other countries also developed more active states after the Second World War. However, the transformation did not happen as a revolution; it was more as a large number of incremental innovations in a row. Nevertheless, the idea of a state that should actively contribute to giving all citizens a decent life was a radical innovation, and involved a restructuring of the whole society.

Many of the large-scale welfare innovations that we today take for granted, such as social insurance, health insurance and family policy, were created during the 1900s. They were developed in order to tackle poverty and other social problems in many industrialized countries (Andersen and Elm Larsen 2004). These reforms could be considered to be radical innovations since they affected large segments of society. Due to different contextual conditions, different welfare systems evolved in different directions (Pierson and Castles 2006). Innovations at the meso level are about enhancing organizations' capacity to innovate. This can be done in public, private and third sector organizations.

Innovations at the micro level focus on engaging with individual citizens and neighbourhoods. These innovations are driven by the needs of citizens. One challenge is to take successful innovations at the micro level and to scale them up. In order to do so, they need to be transferrable and applicable in new contexts. When an innovation is diffused and imported to a new setting, it is important that there are entrepreneurs who can translate the innovation to fit the local context by adaptation. It can be difficult for an individual to incorporate a new innovative practice without having the approval of their organization (Rogers 2003). Institutional entrepreneurs can have such a role to encourage others to adopt new practices.

Institutional entrepreneurs can either create new institutions or change existing ones. Research on institutional entrepreneurs has taken different starting points; some studies mainly look at the importance of individual entrepreneurs while others put a larger emphasis of entrepreneurship as a collective process (Hardy and Maguire 2008). An important point that Hardy and Maguire highlight is that key actors are often embedded within the institutional arrangements, which can make it difficult for them to envision new ways of doing things (Hardy and Maguire 2008). The actors who have the power to initiate change have neither the opportunity nor the motivation to do so, because they have too much to gain from maintaining existing structures. Meanwhile, actors on the periphery might have many innovative ideas but not the power to implement them. It is easier to introduce new innovations in newly created markets than to do so in organizational fields that have matured. One reason for this is that generally accepted values and norms have not yet had time to develop into clear patterns that can be mimicked (Hardy and Maguire 2008, p. 204).

User-driven innovation

User-driven innovation has become a common concept in developing technological products and services (von Hippel *et al.* 2011). Users have genuine experience of the products, interfaces or technologies and they can discover problems that can be resolved. Research shows that users often contribute directly to the innovation process and that they are often the innovators of new services or products (von Hippel 2005). Translated to the field of social services, it is important to acknowledge users' first-hand experience of the services provided. "Users" refers not only to individual service users, but also to the organizations and institutions that use the services in one way or another. Welfare and human services have to operate in an environment with high demands and conflicting interests. As organizations, they have to adapt to existing trends and very often they emulate strategies and models from other organizations. In this respect, the concept of open innovation has been used to focus on the importance of external actors in developing innovations (Chesbrough 2003).

Personalization is another concept that feeds into the discussion on service user involvement and innovation. It is a contested concept since it is connected to the personalization of public services. The individual is held responsible for his or her own actions and situations. This view of an active citizen creates certain conditions for the encounter between the individual and the human service organizations (Mik-Meyer and Villadsen 2013).

The whole idea of the welfare service user as a consumer can be contested since the freedom of choice can be questioned. A consumer has the opportunity to choose between different services that he or she can pay for. The consumer can also choose not to consume at all, or not to buy different forms of services or products. Welfare users, however, are very often forced to accept the services given, or have very limited opportunity to choose different services within the welfare system (Salonen 1998).

Adopting a user-driven approach in social welfare and human services can help to create services that have a greater impact on the problems that they are intended to solve. Service users' own experiences can guide the development of new methods and services and they can highlight issues that have a counter-effect. Very often only small changes need to be made to make a service more effective. Sometimes, however, the whole way of working needs to be revolutionized. The dilemma with service users' own experiences is that this kind of knowledge can be difficult to translate into general use. This kind of knowledge is "sticky":

> We define the stickiness of a given unit of information in a given instance as the incremental expenditure required to transfer that unit of information to a specified locus in a form usable by a given information seeker. When this cost is low, information stickiness is low; when it is high, stickiness is high.
>
> (von Hippel 1994, p. 430)

Service design: planning from service users' perspective

As a professional activity, service design is relatively new. In 2001, Livework and Engine Service Design started their businesses as service design consultants, and were the first firms on the market in Europe (Polaine *et al.* 2013).

Service design has its origins in industry design, but has been adapted to the fact that we are now living in service societies. Attention is given to the quality of the service, as it is developed through the interaction between service users and providers. Service design can be both tangible and intangible. Service designers have been used in connection with marketing and sales in private business. Today they are also engaged in developing, improving and redesigning public services.

The pioneers from Livework state that "[S]ervice design is about designing with people and not just for them, and it is here that it differs from classic user-centered design and much of marketing" (Polaine *et al*. 2013, p. 41). They stress that "people" here means not only service users, but also the front-line staff among the providers, because of their knowledge about the services. Designers have contributed to innovation by involving service users, through multidisciplinary teams, and by using visualization skills (Wetter-Edman 2014).

The relation between service innovation and service design can be rather confusing, but we propose to see service design as a toolbox of methods and techniques for the realization of service innovations, while service innovations can be realized without designers. A key point for designers is to understand the behaviours, needs and motivations of service users, and then construct services accordingly. They are more concerned with in-depth understanding than with drawing statistical conclusions about opinions measured through surveys. It can be described as the difference between insight research and market research, where the designers are less interested in the statistical "truths" (Polaine *et al*. 2013).

In public services, designers are used in many different fields, such as transport and health services. In the field of transport, for instance, they try to understand service users' needs and behaviours, and design the timetables and the infrastructure using these insights. Seen from the outside, the need for this elementary knowledge could be regarded as common sense. It can be seen as a vital part of good leadership to construct services according to the wishes of their users. However, we know only too well that many other demands, both from professionals and politicians, can take precedence over the perspectives of service users, and many professionals act on behalf of users, because they are experts on users' situations. This is well documented in health services. In Norway, for instance, designers are contributing to reducing the waiting time for women diagnosed with breast cancer from two months (between diagnosis and treatment). You do not need to be suffering from breast cancer yourself to understand that such a long wait is awful. Today people have started to see this as unacceptable; they do not accept that the needs of the system, or the professionals, should have priority.

There are many reasons for this public awakening; user-engaged movements, more competent service users and perhaps also the political turn (NPM) that sees people as customers may all have contributed.

The conclusion of this section is that service designers have contributed to focusing on the needs of service users, and from this angle have contributed to many innovations both in the design of commercial services and in the public sector. Since service design is a relatively new perspective and way of thinking, and since it has only recently been offered as an academic discipline at all levels of public service, we may expect that there is more to come.

Spontaneous mobilization, design labs and bottom-up initiatives

Globalization has affected many aspects of life and changed social relationships in many ways. An important innovation is the internet and the new and different forms of communication via social media. The result is that news and ideas now have the opportunity to spread at an immense speed. In early June 2014, for instance, a man took a photo of anti-homeless floor studs that had been placed outside an apartment block in London. The picture was put on Twitter and spread rapidly, first on social media and soon thereafter in the mainstream media. The protests and negative attention that the anti-homeless spikes caused resulted in their removal. This example shows how quickly a news story can spread and how people can engage spontaneously with issues that they find problematic and that are seen as exclusionary practices.

Using design and architecture to prevent the homeless or other marginalized groups from using public space is not a new phenomenon. Different forms of disciplinary architecture have been used for a long time in order to prevent anti-social behaviour and exclude poor people from certain spaces (Knutagård 2009). The spikes represent a moral geography of exclusion, whereby some people do not have access to certain spaces (Philo 1986; Driver 1988; Cresswell 2005; Knutagård 2013). Today's disciplinary architecture of public space can be seen as representing a soft policy of exclusion (Thörn 2011).

A contrast to the disciplinary forms of architecture is the use of design and architecture to shape more inclusive societies. These initiatives are often created from a bottom-up perspective, engaging local communities in the generation of new designs and physical constructions. On a micro scale, artists and designers have also tried to create physical structures that can be used as shelters, but also as a critique of the exclusion of homeless people in today's societies. One example is the Homeless Vehicle Project by Krzysztof Wodiczko (1999). Martinelli (2013) emphasizes that "the socially innovative potential of bottom-up mobilization in mainstream circles can work to obscure the rolling back of the welfare state" (p. 346).

The increased interest in innovations can be seen in several EU-funded projects. One of the more recent projects is called Welfare Innovations at the Local Level in Favour of Cohesion (WILCO) (Evers *et al.* 2014). Many of the cases that are used to illustrate the development of socially innovative strategies involve community work and bottom-up initiatives. Some of these initiatives focus on single parents (especially mothers) and on childcare provision. Many projects focus on unemployment. A large number of the innovative strategies presented concern different forms of housing initiative. Some relate to self-renovation or self-building practices and others to public rental housing programmes or social housing.

Research on social innovations should be cautious of the risk of renaming practices (Halvorsen *et al.* 2005). This has been evident for Housing First services; renaming a shelter as a Housing First service does not make it a Housing

First service. The same is true for unemployment programmes for vulnerable groups. If a programme does not lead to inclusion or integration into the ordinary labour market, there is a risk that it will end up as a poverty trap for those it was intended to help (Moulaert *et al.* 2013, p. 17).

Another important area for social innovations concerns environmental challenges. The Austrian architect and artist Friedensreich Hundertwasser was a pioneer in creating buildings that were in harmony with their environment. We can clearly see the importance of interconnecting different disciplines when addressing the environmental challenges that humanity is facing. It is about thinking the unthinkable and at the same time using the knowledge of the people who are affected by both the problem and the potential solution. Current examples of innovative solutions to environmental challenges are, for instance, co-housing, community currency and the building of low-carbon communities (Science Communication Unit 2014; Jiang *et al.* 2013).

Organizing service user involvement

Traditionally, third sector organizations (non-governmental organizations, charities, not-for-profit businesses) have been involved in providing services for marginalized groups. These organizations have historically been based on the principle of "us for them". This means that service users themselves have not run the organizations. Instead, we can trace the genealogy of social work back to philanthropic ideals that have now re-emerged in new shapes and forms. New forms of user-led organizations have emerged that are based on the idea of "we for us" (Meeuwisse and Sunesson 1998). In these organizations, the members have their own experience of a certain social problem and it is this experience that gives them the opportunity to be included as members. User-led organizations can construct a platform in order to get members' voices heard.

One innovation at the micro level is the so-called self-help movement. Both AA and Fountain House can be seen as very successful innovations in this regard (Svensson and Bengtsson 2010, p. 191). They were both founded in the US in the 1940s and have now diffused globally (Karlsson 2006; Meeuwisse 1997). Individuals who had their own experiences of alcohol abuse and mental illness built up both movements. We can draw a parallel with the street paper movement, discussed in Chapter 3, where a strong entrepreneur makes it possible for an idea to be widely adopted and accepted by other actors.

Over the past decade, greater attention has been given to social enterprises. The dilemma for many service users with social problems is that they lack the organizational setting necessary to get their voice heard. Social enterprises have become one such organizational structure that can enable, for instance, formerly homeless people to find different forms of employment opportunities (Gidron and Hasenfeld 2012).

Gap-mending pedagogy

Academics within universities can also take an active role in creating a space for user-driven innovations (Mulgan 2012). *Gap-mending pedagogy* is an example of an innovation that intersects the knowledge from academia, social work practice and service users' own experiences (Heule *et al.* forthcoming). The idea was created in 2005 (Denvall *et al.* 2011b). Teachers and researchers at the School of Social Work at Lund University in Sweden applied for money from the European Social Fund (ESF) to develop a 7.5 credit course entitled "Social Change and Social Mobilization". It was a collaboration between the School of Social Work and Basta, a user-led social enterprise in Sweden. The key ingredient in the course is the establishment of a platform for mutual learning in which the different experiences of the service users and the social work students are integrated. Service users from different service user organizations are recruited as students (with experiences of mental health problems, substance abuse, homelessness, disability, etc.). Many do not have any prior qualifications that would enable them to take a university course. The course is organized as a commissioned course and the service users who pass it also receive credits. Both the "internal" and the "external" students work together in order to create innovative solutions to urgent social problems within welfare and human services.

For many of the social work students, this course gives them a new perspective on social work and they are able to dismantle some of the preconceptions that they had of different service users. The same is true for the service users. Often they have a very negative and stereotyped image of social workers and social services in general. The course makes it possible for the students and service users to meet on equal terms. Over the years, hundreds of service users have passed the course and are now active in many settings. In his final paper on the course, one of the students, who had a long experience of homelessness behind him, concluded:

> The course has meant that I did something "real" for the first time in 25 years. It has been a useful experience and I have in this way been included in a social community …. I have been able to break my usual pattern and I know now that I can do this. Empowerment gives me the tools to manage not to end up in isolation and to keep me away from drugs. User participation, for me, is being able to work with other types of people and situations in everyday life, which I had not previously done so well maybe. I now know that my opinions are worth something and that people listen to what I have to say. My desire is to be able to convey some of my experiences in life, good and bad, to young people so that they do not end up where I ended up. Best of all was the positive energy that all students gave us service users. Who could have dreamed this one year ago, when I lay shivering in my tent?

In 2013, the municipality of Malmo, the third largest city in Sweden, initiated a project on service user influence within the social service sector. Many of the participating service users had taken the course and could now use their experience in a real social change project. This does not mean that the project in Malmo works without problems, but it does show how small-scale innovative practices can feed into organizational settings that might have systemic consequences in the long run. How it will turn out is, of course, an empirical question.

One interesting challenge is that the course concept has not yet diffused to other universities in Sweden, though it has spread to several other countries such as Norway, Denmark, Germany and the UK. In all countries, the concept has been adapted to local contexts, but key entrepreneurs have been a precondition. The diffusion of the innovation was made possible by a collaborative project funded by the EU-funded Leonardo da Vinci programme Development of Innovation within the Lifelong Learning Programme (EACEA 2013). A network was created, PowerUs (www.powerus.se), with the main goal of developing new innovative methods for service user involvement in social work education.

Bovaird (2007) stresses that "Coproduction is not a panacea" (p. 856). While user-led innovations have been prominent within technological developments, the welfare service system has been much more sluggish and less interested in facilitating the inclusion of service users in developments. Service users have been engaged in the planning processes of different forms of services, but it is more difficult to build mutual relationships when it comes to the individual's encounter with the welfare organization. It is often the direct contact between the service user and the welfare system that is the most problematic to change, and it is very difficult to divide the power equally between the two parties to create a more emancipatory relationship in social work practice (Beresford and Croft 2001; Mik-Meyer and Villadsen 2013). Beresford and Croft (2001) state that:

> The experience of service users and their organizations is that such exercises have very limited effects in improving their lives and services, while making significant demands upon them. Many service users and their organizations report a strong sense of consultation fatigue, of being consulted out. In this key sense, with a consumerist approach to user involvement, services can be seen still to be provider- rather than user-led.
>
> (p. 296)

There is a risk of the illusion of inclusion. When service users are invited to attend different meetings or to be part of projects, their involvement can be merely symbolic rather than having a real effect on the decisions made (Rønning and Solheim 1998). At the same time, it is important not to see user-led organizations or user-led initiatives as being positive by definition.

Housing First as an innovation

We will use Housing First as an example of an innovation at the meso level, but it can also partly be seen as an innovation at the micro level. Housing First has been launched internationally as an innovation within social welfare and human services (Busch-Geertsema 2011, 2013). Innovations within the public sector follow a slightly different innovation process than, for instance, technological innovations. Innovations that are diffused in the private market have profit maximization as a driving force. This is not the case within the public sector, even though cost efficiency is seen as an important objective. As a case study, Housing First highlights the organizational level and illustrates how the innovation process may also have consequences at micro and macro levels.

Housing First is described as a philosophy, a programme, a method and a model. The origin of the concept is attributed to Sam Tsemberis, who founded the non-profit organization Pathways to Housing in 1992 in New York. Housing First services should, according to the Pathways to Housing model, be based on the following eight principles:

1   housing as a basic human right;
2   respect, warmth and compassion for all clients;
3   a commitment to working with clients for as long as they need;
4   scattered-site housing and independent apartments;
5   separation of housing and services;
6   consumer choice and self-determination;
7   a recovery orientation;
8   harm reduction.

(Tsemberis 2010, p. 18)

The basic idea in Housing First services is that housing is a precondition to ending homelessness. This might be seen as common sense to many people, but many of the strategies that are used to combat homelessness have been based on the principle that homeless people need to "learn how to live" before they can get a house of their own. This model is sometimes referred to as the treatment first model. In this model, homeless people need to be "housing-ready" and qualify through a housing staircase (Sahlin 1996; Knutagård 2009), and the lack of housing is not always seen as the real problem. Accessing these services often requires total abstinence from drugs and alcohol. In Housing First services, there is no prerequisite for abstinence; instead, there is a clear separation between support and housing. This separation makes Housing First services a radically new way of working with the homeless in many contexts. As an innovation, it is of interest that the model was designed as an alternative to treatment first services. Another key factor is that the service user is seen as the expert and that he or she should have the freedom to choose the services that he or she needs. Mulgan (2006) states: "Some of the most effective methods for cultivating social innovation start from the presumption that people are competent interpreters of their own lives and competent solvers of their own problems" (p. 150).

In a recent study, it was concluded that the success of the Housing First model could be attributed to the trusting relationships that were established between the formerly homeless people and the support workers (Knutagård and Kristiansen 2013). More research is needed on how this kind of relationship can be created, but what is relevant here is the concept of trust. Many of the formerly homeless people had a strong mistrust towards social services due to their past experiences. When they entered the programme, many of the service users did not think that the Housing First service would be any different to the other forms of homelessness services that they had been using. In their past experiences, a relapse resulted in them being thrown out of programmes. When the Housing First support workers told the service users that abstinence was not required in order to get a flat on their own, they were reluctant to believe the support workers. When the formerly homeless people discovered that they could actually tell the support workers about their problems without any sanctions, they had an opportunity to start along the road to recovery. Very strong and close relationships were established between the service users and the support workers. The service users also became ambassadors for the project, telling their friends about the positive aspects of the service. A key point of interest is whether the trust established at a micro level can also affect the service users' perception of the social service as a whole. Is it possible to organize the work within the general housing services in a community so that trusting relationships can be the norm, rather that the usual mistrust (Kramer and Cook 2004; Misztal 1996)? If so, there is a potential for scaling up an innovation that is co-produced with the service users.

Innovations within the public sector are connected to social change and that is a main feature of social work practice. Despite this fact, there is not much research on social innovations in social welfare and human services (Mulgan 2006). Many innovations that have emerged from both civil society and the public sector have been organizational or administrative in their nature (Halvorsen *et al.* 2005). It is uncommon today to find large-scale strategies that are intended to solve social problems at a systemic level. With regard to Housing First, the model has been part of national strategies in many countries, such as the US and Canada and in Nordic countries such as Finland and Denmark. Housing First is a small-scale innovation, the effectiveness of which has been tested by the EU (Pleace 2012). The very idea is that these effective methods can thereafter be spread and implemented nationally. Research has shown that technical, political and financial aid are important conditions in the first stages of the innovation process (Alvord *et al.* 2004). The large-scale political homelessness strategies in, for instance, the Finnish programme can thus be seen as important for the spread of Housing First in other countries in Europe. The governance that EU programmes have on social innovation can also be seen as an important condition behind the increased political interest in so-called housing-led approaches in Europe.

The diffusion of Housing First can also be related to a larger trend in society. From a rational perspective on the social policy process, the logic is that successful small-scale pilots can be scaled up. Unfortunately, there is a tendency for successful pilots to be abandoned due to lack of funding or when the projects end (Denvall *et al.* 2011a; Alvord *et al.* 2004). There is a risk that specific social innovations become selective interventions for a very narrow target group, rather than part of a more general strategy directed towards a larger group. One conclusion from the work done on Housing First in many countries is that it is very difficult to see how these small-scale pilots can affect the overall homelessness services in a country.

The body of research that shows the positive effects of Housing First is now drawn not only from the US but also from several countries in Europe. These results suggest that Housing First seems to work in very different contexts, even though there have been local adaptations to the model. Perhaps the greatest success of the Housing First model has been the high housing retention rates (over 90 per cent in some services). The principle of housing as a human right can be seen as a relatively radical idea, especially in the light of the fact that the model emerged in the US.

Innovations in public services do not follow a linear process but rather a spiral motion, in which failures are common. These failures can lead to new ideas and proposals that can be launched and developed. In earlier chapters, we touched upon the definition of innovations as radical or incremental changes. Radical innovations will dissolve the previous mindset or system in favour of a new way of doing things. Radical innovations may thus have enormous consequences for our social behaviour (Alvord *et al.* 2004). The same goes for technological innovations such as railways, electricity and the internet. They have radically changed our conceptions of both time and space (Florida 2002; Friedland and Boden 1994). Although incremental innovations are more controllable, it appears as though it is large-scale radical innovations that have really changed our society. We can compare these radical transformations with Kuhn's ideas about paradigm shift. These shifts can only happen when there is extensive criticism of the old way of working, so that a new system can take its place.

The first stage of an innovation process is that a problem is identified. Second, a new solution is proposed, and third, the new idea is tested as a pilot or prototype. What we can see in relation to the issue of homelessness is that its return as a pressing social problem created a need to invent new solutions. Many social workers felt a sense of resignation since they did not have any other help to offer other than placing homeless people in temporary shelters. This solution tended to be their first remedy (Knutagård 2009). Research had also shown the link between homelessness and health problems (Varney and van Vliet 2008). Another factor was the cost of homelessness. One of the main reasons why Housing First became so popular in the US was that research showed that 10 per cent of the long-term homeless people living in shelters used half of the total number of shelter nights (Kuhn and Culhane 1998). If this group could be targeted and properly housed, the costs could be reduced by half (Alvord *et al.* 2004). A housing shortage and landlord requirements for getting a lease are, however, factors that make the introduction of a Housing First initiative much harder.

When the discourse on homelessness changed and it was regarded not as an individual problem but as an issue that was dependent on structural, organizational and individual factors, a "window of opportunity" opened up in the field.

These windows of opportunities are limited in time and space. It is necessary for entrepreneurs to identify these opportunities and take advantage of them (Kingdon 2003; Hardy and Maguire 2008).

During the testing of Housing First Europe, there was still some resistance from the organizational environment since there were no successful pilots to use as good examples in a European context. We know that uncertainty spurs mimetic strategies. At this stage, it is therefore important for policy entrepreneurs to spread and translate the innovation to local contexts, so that it can receive broader acceptance. The key is that the adopters must perceive Housing First as being better than existing approaches (Rogers 2003). However, Mulgan (2006) emphasizes that it is quite rare that those who initiate an innovation also take it to scale. The reason for this is that these two tasks require totally different skills; the former is more about generating creative ideas, whereas the latter is more about creating growth and sustainability.

When innovations become more like everyday practices, they have entered the fourth stage of the innovation process. Housing First has entered this stage in many countries. The media coverage is quite extensive, and the results from different pilots have shown that the method is applicable in many settings and they are therefore used as good examples or success stories. During this stage, it is important for pilots to find sustainable structures.

The hurdle for Housing First now is for it to be scaled up in order to challenge the dominant model within homelessness services. In order to do so, the surrounding organizational landscape has to be ready for change. The organizations' absorptive capacity is central in this development (Cohen and Levinthal 1990).

In the final stage of the innovation process, the innovation is supposed to replace the old ways of thinking and working. In other words, the innovation should become institutionalized. This takes time and often requires that many small innovations together contribute to systemic change. In the US, Housing First has had a major impact on the socio-political discourse. There has been a change from a focus on housing readiness to the view that a house is essential on the road to recovery (Stanhope and Dunn 2011). The most central challenge for systemic change is that innovations that are supposed to solve social problems at a structural level need to change the very system that actually created and perpetuated the problems in the first place (Alvord *et al.* 2004).

Innovations that are systemic or social are often large-scale and affect a large proportion of society, and thus have a big impact. They are widely diffused and sustainable over time, becoming embedded practices that are taken for granted. State reforms are either intended as a universal solution for all, or target specific disadvantaged groups such as unemployed youth, low-income single parents or undocumented immigrants.

Innovations that have the objective of changing society can occur at a local, national, EU or global level. The recent financial crisis has put new pressure on welfare provisions in many countries. Immigration, an ageing population, low birth rates and "environmental deprivation" – "a concept akin to socioeconomic deprivation [which] relates to the presence (e.g., air pollution) or absence (e.g., green space) of physical environmental conditions that might contribute to health differences across areas" (Richardson *et al.* 2013, p. 154) – are just a few examples of the challenges that many countries are facing.

The focus on housing is not a surprise considering the effects that the financial crisis in 2008 had on financial markets around the world. In Europe, it had devastating effects in many countries such as Spain, Ireland, Iceland, Portugal and Greece. The bursting of the property bubble in Spain had terrible consequences for many households; many people were evicted. From a small-scale initiative sprung a large-scale anti-eviction movement.

It is not always easy to solve housing problems with temporary solutions or with different forms of social housing. There is always a risk that housing that is only built for a certain group becomes stigmatized. It also takes time to build new housing. The housing shortage can therefore trigger small-scale social housing projects or self-building initiatives. Self-building initiatives do not have a significant impact on the housing shortage in general, but they can certainly make a difference for the people who have the opportunity to be housed.

Two global challenges are refugee flows and immigration. Solving these issues cannot be done locally; instead, they require new policies and solutions at both the national and international level. There are no quick fixes; instead, strategic and sustainable solutions are necessary. In recent years, there has been growing support for anti-immigration political parties. Immigrants are the people who are most often affected by an economic recession in a country. It can be very difficult for immigrants to gain access to the labour market. For minority groups, such as the Roma, the effects of the financial crisis in Europe have forced many people to try to find work across national borders. Many Roma are victims of stigmatization and social exclusion. A recent trend has been the criminalization of begging in the urban landscape.

Vitale and Membretti (2013) give us one example of a housing initiative in Italy that, according to the authors, has been innovative. The need that had to be met was for housing solutions for Roma families who were excluded from the housing market. In this case, the actors involved actually managed to provide housing that was not only for Roma families, making the initiative inclusive. The authors also show how a previously stigmatized space can be changed through the use of art. The Roma who were housed were also involved in the building process, learning construction skills and getting paid to do the work. By including the families in the planning process, this can also be seen as a user-driven initiative.

Conclusion

Steve Jobs once said that "it's really hard to design products by focus groups. A lot of times, people don't know what they want until you show it to them" (*Business Week* 1998). This quotation can be seen as provocative in relation to user-driven innovation. That said, the quotation also illustrates the delicate relationship between different forms of knowledge and perspectives. The creation and implementation of new innovations is not a one-man job. Even though we can identify hero entrepreneurs, the institutions and resources that surround them are of the utmost importance. There is a great need to develop supportive structures for service user involvement and user-led innovations within social welfare and human services. Many of the existing structures are adapted to technological innovations. One of the areas that is underdeveloped is funding for research on social innovations. Even though there is a large amount of funding from the EU, it is important to see EU programmes as political projects. At the same time, it is also important to reflect on the supportive systems that are necessary. In many cases, there might not be a need for new institutions, but the focus on innovations within social welfare and human services has created a new niche for different incubators and hubs.

Is it possible to put new wine in old bottles? Can innovations such as Housing First, for instance, radically change the way homelessness services are organized? Based on organizational institutionalism, we can see some key challenges to changing existing institutions (Eriksson-Zetterquist 2009; Jönsson *et al.* 2011).

Creating a new organization in order to solve a problem has in itself become an institutionalized practice. Organizations also have to be constructed in a certain way in order to be legitimate. They are dependent on their environment for both funding and acceptance. This dependency also creates similarity. It is not an easy task to change the expectations surrounding homelessness services. Homeless shelters are often seen as the right place for the homeless to stay. Giving homeless people apartments of their own can trigger moral judgements, and to implement new solutions in social welfare, it can be necessary to combat moral attitudes. We take for granted that the aim of social welfare and human services is to solve a problem for a vulnerable group. "People must be the heart of the service" is a basic principle for service designers (Polaine *et al.* 2013). Workable solutions need the participation of the groups that they are intended to help. That is true for innovations at all levels. The proof is in the pudding, and if it works for service users, it is probably also the best value for the rest of society. By contrast, creating services that users do not want can trigger resistance.

7   Obstacles to innovation

The future cannot be predicted, it has to be created.

(Ridderstråle and Nordstrøm 2004)

In this chapter, we will discuss some of the obstacles to innovation in organizations. Innovative work is an intentional challenge to the established way of performing tasks. Not surprisingly, counter-forces are mobilized, as already mentioned. However, there are many other obstacles built into the structures and our way of behaviour too. Innovation is a way of thinking and a culture, not a particular technique or method, or a specific project. To innovate is therefore to fight a constant battle to overcome what we have believed in before. The outcomes may not be what we expected, and may even be counter-productive with respect to our stated goals.

The outcomes may be different or the opposite of what we expected

The epigraph above refers especially to the private sector, but is also relevant to the public sector. NPM was introduced as an innovation in the public sector, and this way of adopting ideas and models from the private sector fits well into our definition of innovations. Even if NPM is not a well-defined phenomenon, the versions we find in different countries are sufficiently uniform to discuss the common core (Christensen and Lægreid 2002). NPM united two strong ideological trends from the post-war period. The first trend consisted of economic theory in which the main focus was to see people as rational actors (public choice theory), and the second trend was theories of leadership in which attention was given to the importance of leadership (managerialism) (Hood 1991; Klausen 2001).

A premise of public choice theory is that the market is the most effective distributor of resources in most social arenas. The interaction here is based on supply and demand; consumers demand a product and suppliers compete to deliver it. Perfect competition is assumed, which implies that suppliers go into the market as long as they can make a reasonable profit. However, if too many suppliers compete, the profit will shrink and some suppliers may decide to withdraw. The system is said to be self-regulating. The consumer is king in this model; he or she chooses the preferred product based on a total assessment of quality and price.

As an alternative to a model in which bureaucrats (or professionals) were seen as the rulers, this model was perceived by politicians and many service users as an improvement. However, there are a number of conditions that have to be met if the model is to work in the distribution of, for instance, health services. A basic condition is the existence of a sufficient number of suppliers to make sure that there is real competition. Then the consumers must have enough information about what they get for the price to be able to make their choice. This is difficult in the relation between lay people and professionals such as medical doctors, because the reason we visit the doctor is that he or she knows more about the problem than us.

We will illustrate the situation for the NPM approach with the purchaser–provider model used in elderly care in many countries, already mentioned briefly in Chapter 2. The model is a good illustration of the market logic in welfare services. By specifying and tendering the services, the intention is that competition will give the best combination of price and quality in care. The condition of a significant number of providers may not be met, the customers (the elderly) are not all able to make an informed choice, and, since the municipalities also have to pay for the service, they are the purchasers on behalf of the elderly.

In the market, goods and services are exchanged for money, and many transactions take place smoothly and informally. However, for larger transactions formal contracts are used, making it clear what each of the two parties is obliged to do, and making it possible for each party to take the other to court if those obligations are not met. These contracts are built on the logic of distrust; the other party wants to cheat you and will use every opportunity to do so if it is not mentioned in the contract. This model has replaced the established relations between professionals and clients (service users). These relations have been normally based on trust; professional ethics were an imperative for professionals to do their best for the other party. We can see the "old" model as leadership based on common values, and it has, all in all, been an efficient model. A model with external controllers has to be more costly.

Furthermore, as mentioned, the system will be rigid because the level of service that the individual will receive is defined in advance. When we are old and frail, our situation and needs can change rapidly. Contracts can be rewritten for an individual, but it is more bureaucracy and paperwork compared to a situation in which a professional can make the decision on the spot. The purchaser can control the provider through controls and reported negative deviations (tasks not done or done wrongly). For the providing company and its employees, the rule must be that they should not do more than is expected by the contract. For a nurse, it is sometimes difficult not to meet an obvious need. However, if he or she goes beyond what is specified in the contract, the profit margin will be reduced or lost. This situation is what we can call a positive deviation; it is good for service users but expensive for providing firms. The use of tendering makes the system more bureaucratic and rigid, quite contrary to the intentions behind it.

When we intervene and innovate in a large and complex system, it is difficult to know what kind of interaction effects we will trigger, as mentioned by Popper (1945). NPM was, like many other political innovations, driven more by ideology than by empirical findings. This can also make it easier to miss the target. To put elderly care out to tender may reduce costs for the services, and in that way achieve one of the stated goals. However, to make the new model workable, it has been necessary to use procedures that make it less flexible and to add costs in other areas. Since the use of market mechanisms was proclaimed as a way to reduce bureaucracy, more bureaucracy is a touchy side-effect. Formalizing the provision and delivery of services through the use of contracts was an unforeseen but necessary step for realizing the innovation.

When innovations prevent further innovations

If we see innovation as a way of thinking, we have the difficult mental task of remaining eternally dissatisfied, even when an innovation seems to be very successful. When those who implement an innovation evaluate it as a success and service users agree, it is easy to take a break. This is what service users expect; they are satisfied, and can react negatively if we try to move on. Most of us prefer a well-functioning model today rather than an unproven alternative. We have a number of slogans that express this preference, such as "Never change a winning team". In elections, different versions have been used as slogans. In 1957, the conservative West German Chancellor Konrad Adenhauer won a landslide victory with the slogan "Keine Experimente" ("No experiments"). Social democratic parties, when they have been in power, have used similar slogans. In Norway, the Social Democratic Party stayed in power after the elections in 1993, using the slogan "Trygghet for framtida" ("Confidence for the future"). Mentally, people are opposed to change if they do not experience the present situation as one that demands it.

When innovations involve the large-scale reorganization of established structures, people need time to adapt to the new reality. Waves of changes can make people – both service users and employees – angry. Nevertheless, we know that if a solution is good at time T1, it will be outdated at time T2, simply because our surroundings and options change. It can be a delicate balance. When we get credit for an innovation, we feel inclined to stop and enjoy it. However, as Willie Nelson sang, we have to be "on the road again". "Restless creativity" is the recipe (Ridderstråle and Nordstrøm 2004, p. 267).

The mental barriers to innovation are important to keep in mind. However, we have also built in organizational obstacles to further innovations. Some ways of organizing public–private partnerships (PPPs) can illustrate this.

A PPP often means that a private firm takes responsibility for developing a public project (such as a road or a hospital) and operates it over a long period (20–30 years), during which time they get their money and some profit back through tolls or other forms of repayment. How profitable a project is depends on the contract in each case. There has been much discussion about the economy in these projects, and in some cases, there have been protests from service users. One famous UK case is the bridge to the Isle of Skye. When the bridge was completed in 1995, the ferries to the island were stopped and the only way to go was via the bridge. The islanders found it too expensive; the deal made with the owners (a US company) would give the company back double the construction costs over the course of the contract, and this had to be paid by the islanders because of the monopoly situation (Monbiot 2000). The service users protested against the implementation of the innovation. The disputes about costs are not our concern here; our focus is on the consequences for further innovations. The bridge, built to replace the ferry, was an innovation. However, during the term of the contract, the government could not make arrangements that would threaten the contract with the constructors.

To take another example, in Sydney the government gave a Hong Kong-based syndicate the responsibility for building a new tunnel under the city to relieve some of the street traffic. However, the Sydneysiders found the tolls too high and many chose options other than the tunnel. The contract between the government and the syndicate was secret, but after a while it became known that the government had guaranteed that a given number of cars would pass through the tunnel every day. So when people started to take other roads, the government had to close down these alternatives; if they did not, they would have to pay the syndicate a large compensation fee. The tunnel grew into a national scandal in the autumn of 2005, with daily comments in Sydney's largest newspaper the *Sydney Morning Herald*. The government was forced to publish the agreement with the syndicate, which also contained a paragraph in which the government promised that they would not construct any collective transport solutions that could compete with the tunnel for the next 30 years. An editorial published in the *Sydney Morning Herald* on 22 October 2005 summed up the lessons to be learned. The first was openness; those who are affected by a decision should be informed. The second was the need for flexibility and the opportunity to find better and improved solutions.

Both the service user focus and the need for an unlocked future are important in innovation. We do not know what will happen in the future, but we know that both needs and possible solutions may be different from what they are now. Using PPPs in the way described in these two cases is therefore a counter-productive way of innovating, because they limit new options. The case of the Sydney tunnel is also politically sensitive because the PPP is a hindrance to better environmental solutions, as it forces people to use cars.

A zero-mistake culture

Introductory books about innovation and creativity underline that in a creative setting there must be high tolerance for mistakes. Failures can lead the way to important innovations. In one of these books, we can read:

We have got to fail faster to learn quicker and succeed sooner. "Failure is just part of the culture of innovation. Accept it and become stronger", advises Albert Yu, senior vice-president at Intel. In Silicon Valley, failure is not a black dot – it is a badge of achievement.

(Nordstrøm and Ridderstråle 1999, p. 193)

In the same book, the authors note that the only way not to fail is not to try.

Opposed to this, we have had a management-led programme in industry called Zero Defects, defined as a management tool aimed at the reduction of defects through prevention. It is directed towards motivating people to prevent mistakes by developing a constant, conscious desire to do the job right the first time (Halpin 1966). It was mostly used from 1964 until 1970 in US industry, but had a renaissance in the 1990s, when it was more a performance goal than a programme. The programme could be used by all types of enterprises, but was mostly adopted by firms that produced large volumes of components.

The idea behind Zero Defects was that it is cheaper to make something right the first time, than to have it corrected later. Quality is seen as conformance to requirements. A detailed specification is needed; if that is followed, the product will be without defects. That is in itself a quality standard.

The model does not seem to be very useful if we try to transfer it to welfare services, in which individual treatment is required and the "product" is created through interaction with service users. Furthermore, we can imagine that, as a model for leadership, the Zero Defects principles will have little tolerance for risk-taking and failures. The model has few advocates in today's service society, but it may have a cousin in modern management theory. Together with NPM, we have burdensome control regimes in the public sector. Employees have to report what they do and have done, and manuals are established to ensure the achievement of quality. The introduction of a market logic in services, and the use of contracts, has created a paperwork regime. Leadership by indicators is another source of rigidity. A stronger focus on service user rights has worked the same way because it is now possible to exert control and ensure that the providers have done what they have promised and get paid for. The US model, in which professionals can be taken to court if they have done anything irregular, may also have been influential. Regularity is defined by the manuals. The model leaves little space for professional discretion. Regulations have penetrated society to such an extent that it has been labelled "the regulatory state" (Majone 1994). Majone (1994) states that "privatisation and deregulation have created the conditions for the rise of a regulatory state to replace the dirigiste state of the past" (p. 77). He explains it as follows: "[R]eliance on regulation – rather than public ownership, planning or centralised administration – characterises the methods of the regulatory state" (p. 2). Control arrangements are a condition for the rise of a regulatory state (Veggeland 2009).

A move from direct to indirect leadership – leadership "at arm's length" – has prompted the establishment of control agencies. In many countries, we now find separate agencies for the doers and the controllers within the same field.

In health services, we have both a directorate for the executive part and an agency for supervision; it is the same for air traffic control, and other fields. The organization of the public sector varies from country to country, but we find some of these patterns in many countries. In Europe, the EU can be seen as contributing to standardization through making generally applicable decisions and controlling their implementation.

The development described above may seem to be rather paradoxical. In business, the slogan is "innovate or die", where Kodak is used as an example of a company that went from being a leading producer to bankruptcy because they did not innovate fast enough. The public sector has been innovated to be more like private business, but has developed a regulatory control regime with little tolerance for failures. It is no controversial conclusion to state that this model is counter-productive for innovation.

One effect of the regulatory state is more standardization. This will be discussed in the next section.

Standardized and evidence-based services

Standardization was mentioned as long ago as in Greek mythology. Procrustes invited travellers to have a night's rest in a bed with the unique property that its length fitted everyone who came to sleep. His method was to adapt the guest to the bed; those who were too short were stretched and those who were too long had their legs amputated. In the EU today, when we have standards for the length of a cucumber, we can see some of the same principles at work.

Standardization is fundamental for living together in societies. We need common rules and a common language to interact. A standard is a type of rule, telling us how to behave in a certain situation. When we are driving our car on the roads, for instance, we have to trust that the other drivers will adhere to the same rules that we do; when we go abroad, we are grateful that the traffic signs are standardized; and when we come from Continental Europe to the UK by car, we wish they had standardized even more and drove on the right-hand side of the road. In daily life, we can want both more and less standardization. Microsoft's dominant role within software manufacture has contributed to a standard used by the majority of people, making it possible to communicate worldwide, and we see the problems with software that is not compatible. Within health care, we still have lots of examples of systems that do not communicate with each other. This is not efficient and can make providing adequate treatment difficult. On the other hand, we do not want "one size fits all" all of the time. People can want a restaurant that is unique, rather than a burger chain; the same goes for clothes, houses, etc.

There are many good arguments for standardization (Brunsson and Jacobsson 1998). It is effective for the translation of information and crucial for co-ordination. It also makes our daily lives easier, and (we believe) more safe. If we trust standards for house and bridge construction, for instance, then we feel safe when we are crossing a bridge or buying a new home. It is also argued that standardization means that the best solution will be chosen. This is because the possible solutions are evaluated by professionals. However, power can also contribute to these choices.

We can conclude that standardization is a basic necessity for our daily lives, and particularly for international trade, travelling and communication. However, in many fields and in practical work, there is ongoing discussion about how far standardization should be taken. Rigidity is a consequence of too much rule-oriented behaviour. Some flexibility can make our daily lives run more smoothly. "Standardized flexibility" is the balance we strive for, whereby no recipe is given in advance (Røhnebæk 2014).

Standards are developed in many arenas and by different means. In hierarchies, the standards are set by the people at the top; in the market, through communication and agreements; and in international policy committees, through bargaining. A special form of standardization is the internalization of norms; we grow up in a family and a society and are socialized to a particular understanding of the world and to particular values that we should follow. Some of these norms are built-in rules and laws. Religions, and especially religious leaders in their interpretations of holy texts, have been important for the standardization of norms.

In the Western world today, professionals are more important than religious leaders in deciding standards. Today, the claim for evidence-based practices in different fields is an important driving mechanism for standardization. Furthermore, it is important for the development of welfare services in general, and for the possibility of innovating in these services.

"Evidence-based" has been defined in many different ways, but we will use the following definition, particular to social work:

> evidence-based practice rests on the accumulation of evidence over time studied systematically through knowledge reviews of empirical research or, in its purest "gold standard" sense, meta-analysis of experimental randomized controlled trial studies.
>
> (Gray *et al.* 2009, p. 2)

Evidence-based practice is probably most developed in medicine, and most of us prefer to be treated in a way that is documented as the best. However, the claim for evidence-based practices has also been made in other fields, such as nursing and social work (Timmermans and Berg 2003; Gray *et al.* 2009). The work on evidence-based practice strives towards establishing best practices. Here, both the content and methods can be disputed. Critics have compared the work on evidence-based practice in medicine to scientific management (Taylorism) and the McDonaldization of society (Timmermans and Berg 2003) and characterized it as a "fundamentalist cult with evangelical tendencies" (Charlton 1997).

Our aim is not to enter into the debate about evidence-based practice in general or about how far it should be taken, but to pinpoint that it is a very relevant aspect of the standardization work in social welfare and human services. From the point of view of innovation, it is important to note that all efforts to establish best practices are based on past experience. Innovation, by contrast, is a search for new practices, for the next practice (Jensen *et al.* 2008). Of course, we can say that all future practices are to some extent based on our former experiences. Nevertheless, it is the difference between looking out of the windscreen or in the rear-view mirror when we drive. A best practice is "inside the box", whereas inventions and innovations are "outside the box", to use popular terminology. Standardization and best practice thinking can be a real challenge for innovative work. We do not want to ignore existing knowledge, but some established truths have to be challenged. Maybe we can find some comfort in a quotation from Einstein: "The important thing is not to stop questioning. Curiosity has its own reason for existing" (Einstein, quoted by Harris 1995).

Some other obstacles

Measurable goals and indicators

To be a member of an organization means working together with others to realize common goals. An important task for the leadership is to ensure that members have the same goals, and that they use their energy towards realizing those goals. In large organizations, the main goal has to be broken down into sub-goals that work for the different units. This can be a complex exercise. "Management by objectives" (MBO) was an attempt to overcome this challenge (Drucker 1954). After a participatory process, the goals could be set. Then activities could be measured against these goals. Measuring the actual performance promoted the use of measurable standards. The limitation here is the same as in social science; important aspects of human behaviour cannot easily be expressed in numbers. As a sign hanging in Einstein's office at Princeton noted, "Not everything that counts can be counted, and not everything that can be counted counts" (Harris 1995).

This wisdom has been accepted in organizational theory, though in practice there has always been some effort to make the activities of an organization measurable, and, with the rise of leadership "at arm's length", this approach was given new energy. However, no one has challenged the truth of Einstein's sign.

What can be measured in an uncontroversial way should be measured, but we must also keep in mind the non-measurable information. It is wise to keep Campbell's (1979) law in mind:

> The more any quantitative social indicator (or even some qualitative indicators) is used for social decision-making, the more subject it will be to corruption pressures and the more apt it will be to distort and corrupt the social processes it is intended to monitor.
>
> (p. 85)

If the use of measurable indicators is dominant in an organization, it can limit the possibilities for innovative activity, both because it restricts the scope for innovative work, and because not all aspects of an innovation can be measured in numbers.

Path dependence

In its most simple form, path dependence means that if we start to think or go in one direction and receive positive feedback on that, we will continue in the same direction, limiting the options for alternative solutions. If we successfully solve two mathematical problems in a row using one particular method, for instance, we will have a tendency to try the same method on a third problem. If we had started out open-minded, this third problem may have been better solved using another approach.

For the study of social issues, we can use a more precise definition: "what happened at an earlier point in time will affect the possible outcomes of a sequence of events occurring at a later point in time" (Sewell 1996, pp. 262–263). Each step in one particular direction makes it more difficult to reverse course, and we get into developmental trajectories (Pierson 2004).

It we decide to install an ICT solution for a large organization, for instance, it is very costly to change our minds if we then find a better solution. A much-used example of the enormous costs of changing course is the use of the QWERTY keyboard. When it was established as a standard, all typewriter manufacturers adopted it, and teaching programmes for touch-typing were developed for this standard. Even though later experiments have proven that an alternative arrangement could be more rational and efficient, it would be difficult to change. Similarly, changing to driving on the right-hand side of the road in the UK would also be costly.

The mental aspect of path dependence is a challenge to innovation, and we know that people with similar backgrounds and educations can follow the same mental paths. Intellectual open-mindedness is not easy, not even within scientific cultures. If we have invested decades of our academic life in teaching and writing based on our own groundbreaking results, it is not easy to accept new findings that prove ours to be wrong. Kuhn (1972) describes this development in science as a change from a pre-paradigmatic to a paradigmatic phase. In the former, established knowledge is challenged by new research findings; in the latter, a new paradigm is established as the best available at the time. This phase will last until the paradigm is challenged by new insights.

The term "technology trajectory" refers to a situation in which a technological development is locked within one trajectory, making it impossible to adapt to ideas from the outside. Technology has been an important driver of innovations in society, and is now also gaining more importance for welfare services. Technologists may be too optimistic about the possibilities that their tools represent, following their trajectory. A sceptic has warned: "Technology doesn't make you less stupid; it just makes you stupid faster" (May, quoted in

Ridderstråle and Nordstrøm 2004, p. 193). On the other side, people working in the caring disciplines, such as nurses, can be critical of technological solutions and reluctant to implement them. Both sides have their own path dependences and the challenge for innovation is to bridge the two. Organizational path dependence can narrow the scope of what seemed to be accepted at first glance, and innovation can challenge the followed path. The Kodak case has taught us that sometimes this may be the only way to survive. Innovators must be a constant threat to established truths and path dependence.

8   Innovation: not easy, but imperative[1]

Rock the boat, but stay in it.

(https://changeday.nhs.uk/healthcareradicals)

From the preceding chapters, the message should be clear: when we try to innovate in services that are mainly a public responsibility, we meet challenges and counter-forces. However, since the environment changes, the public sector also has to change – and it does. Another much-used argument in many countries is that we cannot afford to continue solving problems in the way we have done in the past. This can be seen as part of a political debate about private affluence and public poverty, but we state that this is the perspective of the political majority in many countries, and so it is real in its consequences. And if we accept the Baumol Effect (Baumol and Bowen 1966), according to which services are relatively less efficient than production over time, the public sector, which is service-dominated, will fall behind the private sector in efficiency. The public sector has to innovate to both reduce the gap and meet its objectives adequately. In this final chapter, we discuss some strategies for innovation.

A difficult balance

The epigraph above is from the School for Health and Care Radicals in the UK. If you want to bring about change, you must challenge, but at the same time build confidence so you are listened to; you have to stay in the boat. To rock the boat, you must be a rebel in some sense. Lois Kelly (www.rebelsatwork.com) has drawn a distinction between good and bad rebels. The latter are the troublemakers.

Bad rebels	Good rebels	Bad rebels	Good rebels
Complain	Create	Doubt	Believe
Me-focused	Mission-focused	Energy-sapping	Energy-generating
Pessimistic	Optimistic	Pirates	Navy Seals
Break rules	Change rules	Obsessed	Reluctant
Alienate	Attract	Anger	Passion
Problems	Possibilities		

This distinction may be useful for illustrating not only people's different attitudes when they engage in innovative work, but also how they are considered by others. For other people have the power to define us; even if we do not want to be seen as troublemakers, we may be considered as just that. In sociology, it is called "labelling" when a majority of people define individuals or groups negatively as deviants (Becker 1963).

Another way of taking the sting out of rebelling innovators is collaboration (Selznick 1949). The majority of people respond to the rebels in a positive way, and try to convince them that they actually have the same interests, so it is better for the rebels to collaborate to realize their goals. Then the rebels have to accept the rules of the majority, and become invisible. Radical youth groups in political parties are often confronted with the task of navigating between two ditches: being defined as deviants on the one side, or drowned in the majority on the other.

There is an old African saying that "[I]f you want to go fast, go alone; if you want to go far, go together" (Gore 2007). Since innovations in public services are about getting support, innovators have to go together with others, and innovative work is about convincing others about new solutions, often to old challenges.

In this chapter, we will focus on different ways of creating new solutions together in organizations. One important point of departure should be basic in all innovative work: we have to listen to service users, and learn about their needs and behaviours. This has been mentioned in many chapters, but most thoroughly discussed in Chapter 6. In private business, it has long been proven that successful innovators have a good understanding of users' needs, certainly better than the less successful ones (Rothwell *et al.* 1974). We also know that many of the enquiries to public bodies would not be made if service users had got sufficient and correct information the first time around, from either written material or direct verbal communication. A study in the Swedish Social Security Agency ("Försäkringskassan"), for instance, indicated that 70 per cent of the enquiries received were unnecessary (Quist 2014). This is convincing proof of what we can improve by focusing on service users.

There are many sources of information for people who want to learn more about innovation. Books such as ours are hopefully one source. Academic courses can be useful; innovation has, after all, been an academic discipline for almost 50 years, and much can be learned from previous studies and experiences. However, innovation is also practical work, and people have to learn how to do it themselves. Many books are written to guide people into creative work through exercises. If people are allowed to, and encouraged to be creative, they can contribute; innovation is not only for experts. It is said that an expert team at a toothpaste company discussed how customers could be induced to use more toothpaste. The handyman passed by and proposed widening the opening of the tube. Knowledge and inspiration can also be gleaned through interaction with colleagues, learning from how other people handle their challenges. Conferences, competitions and visits can all be the means of generating new ideas. Inspiration can also be taken from many websites, such as www.rebelsatwork.com and https://changeday.nhs.uk.

If an organization decides to begin a process of stimulating innovation, making the necessary arrangements is a leadership task. Many books have been written about how to conduct this task (Burns and Stalker 1961; Bason 2010; Hartley *et al.* 2008; Tidd *et al.* 2005), and so it will not be discussed further in this text. We will instead concentrate on some collaborative strategies.

Mapping the innovation climate

Ekvall (1996) defines the innovation climate as

> an attribute of the organization, a conglomerate of attitudes, feelings and behaviours which characterizes life in the organization, and exists independently of the perceptions and understandings of the members of the organization.
>
> (p. 105)

For the members at a given time that the climate is a reality, it is not identical to the organizational culture, but is rather a manifestation of the culture. Ekvall developed a 50-item questionnaire, covering ten dimensions. The importance of these dimensions is well tested and documented, and they can also be accepted at face value. They are as follows:

1 *Challenge*: the emotional involvement of the members of the organization in its operations and goals. A high score comes when people experience joy and meaningfulness in their job, and so invest much energy in it.
2 *Freedom*: the independence of behaviour exerted by the people in the organization. A high score comes when people are free to make contacts, handle information and use their initiative. The opposite is a rule-bound and controlling setting.
3 *Idea support*: the ways new ideas are treated. In a supportive climate, which gets a high score, ideas are received in an attentive and supportive way by bosses and colleagues. The opposite is a climate in which fault is found and obstacles are raised.
4 *Trust/openness*: the emotional safety in relationships. When there is a high level of trust and openness (high score), everyone in the organization is comfortable putting forward ideas and opinions. If trust is lacking, people are suspicious, afraid of making mistakes and of having their good ideas stolen.
5 *Dynamism/liveliness*: the eventfulness of life in the organization. In a highly dynamic environment (high score), new things are happening all of the time. The opposite is a setting in which everything operates according to familiar routines or traditions.
6 *Playfulness/humour*: the spontaneity and ease that is displayed. A relaxed atmosphere with jokes and laughter characterizes organizations that get a high score here. Gravity and seriousness are the opposites; in such settings, jokes may even be seen as improper.

7   *Debates*: the occurrence of encounters and clashes between differing view-points, ideas and experiences. Many voices are heard and accepted in an organization that scores highly. The opposite is an environment without debates, in which people follow authoritarian patterns without opposition.

8   *Conflicts*: the presence of conflicts and emotional tensions between people (in contrast to conflicts between ideas). This is the only dimension for which it is best to have a low score. In an organization with a high score, there is a warfare-like situation, and plots and traps are part of daily life. The opposite is a setting in which people have impulse control and psychological insight.

9   *Risk-taking*: the tolerance of risk and uncertainty in the organization. In a high-scoring (high risk-taking) organization, decisions and actions are taken promptly and rapidly, without detailed analysis in advance. Decisions can turn out to be wrong and then reconsidered. In low-scoring organizations, people prefer to "sleep on the matter" or establish a committee to study the issue before making a decision.

10 *Idea time*: the amount of time people can (and do) use for elaborating new ideas. In a high-scoring environment, people can discuss ideas and suggestions that are unplanned. The opposite are settings in which perceived time pressures make thinking outside the schedule impossible.

There is a possible paradox in the last dimension. If a crisis is the trigger for innovation, the latter (low-scoring) setting would be fortunate, while a large amount of idea time can give the misleading impression of control. One answer is that in a situation in which there is a perceived crisis, it is important to save idea time. It does not help to run twice as fast if we run in the wrong direction.

It may be a good idea to reflect on the situation in our own organizations, and even to conduct climate mapping using Ekvall's questionnaire. A shorter version with only graded scores for each dimension can also be useful. Indeed, merely discussing the dimensions may trigger important reflections about the capacity for and barriers to innovation in the organizations in which we work.

The scores for each dimension (except the conflict dimension) should not necessarily be understood as "the higher, the better". The right mix depends on our purpose. For a firm in a creative sector, such as architecture, a high score for nine of the dimensions may be good. Snøhetta, a famous Norwegian architectural firm with offices in Oslo and New York, has won several international competitions, and designed buildings such as the Bibliotheca Alexandrina and one of the towers of the new World Trade Center. Their philosophy is to encourage a collective creativity, without any established departments or reserved desks. They want to have a flow of ideas across disciplines, ages, levels of experience and nations (Hagen 2014). If we work in social welfare, we have many routine tasks to perform; we will be both bureaucratic and creative. Risk-taking should not impose any uncertainty on service users. To find the right mix together may be a valuable exercise for improving an organization's innovative capacity.

Employee-driven innovation

Employee-driven innovation (EDI) means that employees are actively involved in the development of new solutions. It refers to the generation and implementation of novel ideas, originated by a single employee or as a collaborative effort.

We can distinguish between three orders of EDI (Høyrup 2012):

1 *First-order EDI* is a bottom-up process, in which an innovation arises from the everyday cultural practice of the employees.
2 *Second-order EDI* is a mixture of bottom-up and top-down processes. In this case, the management strives to systematize and formalize innovative processes initiated by the employees.
3 *Third-order EDI* is a top-down process in which managers invite employees to become involved and participate in innovative processes.

This differentiation makes it clear that EDI can be organized in many ways, but involving employees is still at the core.

Tidd *et al.* (2005) describe the development of high-involvement innovations (HII) as a journey with five stages. The first stage is the natural or unconscious level of involvement; at the second stage, we find the first serious attempts to mobilize HII; and at the fifth stage, we have a situation in which everyone is fully involved in experimenting and improving things, in sharing knowledge and in creating an active learning organization. This may be the goal, but it is not necessarily easy to realize. In a learning organization, the innovative capacity of the organization is utilized. Organizational learning has been proven to be important for innovation (Cohen and Levinthal 1990; Lundvall 2013).

The involvement of employees can be at any or all stages of the whole chain – from ideas, through prioritization and development, to implementation. Their participation can be organized in different ways. When firms started to use employees' ideas, before the advent of the internet, special "suggestion boxes" were created in some organizations, and their use could be stimulated by awarding bonuses for the best suggestions. Today, these boxes are often replaced by virtual boxes on the web. Facebook has been used as a means by which suggestions can be submitted and sorted into different categories according to how useful they are seen to be, as evaluated by the leader or a special committee. Internal competitions can also be used. "Change days" are used for the mobilization of large groups. The NHS in the UK has been a frontrunner here. The aim of the NHS Change Day is a mass mobilization at the grassroots level of people who work in the NHS or use its services: "doing something better together". The 2014 Change Day was the biggest day of collective action for improvement in the history of the NHS. The invitation was "Pledge, share, do and inspire. To make NHS the best it can be". It triggered 81 separate campaigns and more than 800,000 pledges (https://changeday.nhs.uk).

Organizations that succeed in fostering EDI seem to have some common cultural attributes, such as trust, open-mindedness and the promotion of collaboration. The involvement of employees is important for the diffusion of innovations within an organization (Lundvall 2013). EDI may contribute to improved effectiveness, quality improvements, greater job satisfaction, reduced sickness absence and lower job turnover (Amundsen *et al.* 2011), though how much it contributes to each of the different variables is an empirical question.

"Lean" can be seen as both a special form of incremental innovations and a special form of EDI. Since it is so much practised, it will be discussed in a separate section.

"Lean": a way of improving quality

The term "lean" (slim), or "lean manufacturing", was first coined by Krafcik in 1988. It is now a much-used concept, especially in manufacturing industries, but has also been introduced and used in services. Lean is often connected to tools and techniques such as Six Sigma, Total Quality Management (TQM), Just In Time (JIT) and others. However, lean is first and foremost a way of thinking. The critical starting point is *value*. Value can ultimately only be defined by the customer, and some researchers add that it is only meaningful when it is connected to a specific product that meets the customer's needs. In such cases, it is value-adding work. The opposite is non-value-adding work, which should be kept to a minimum (Womack and Jones 2003). Value is created by the producer; from a customer's perspective, that is why producers exist. The principles of lean were developed in Japanese car manufacturing, and are today closely connected to Toyota's production system (TPS). Here, the gradual elimination of "muda" (waste) is the driving force. Waste is defined by what the customer wants (and is willing to pay for). The aim is to produce that, and no more, without any waste. Waste is reduced as quality improves, while production time and costs are also reduced.

Lean involves continuous improvement work, and improvements can be made in different areas: transport (do we have to search for and transport things we need in the production process more than necessary?), motion (do we move more than needed?), waiting time (do we need to wait for others in the production line?), overproduction (do we produce more than is demanded at the actual time?). Reducing defects is also mentioned, then connecting to the Zero Defects theory. The attention given to transport and motion here can be compared with Taylor's scientific management, treating humans like machines (as caricatured in Charlie Chaplin's Modern Times), but, in contrast to Taylor's human robots, employees engaged in lean work are participating in quality improvement. However, it is a challenge to keep the engagement consistent in a top-down organized (third-order) EDI model. Since lean is a philosophy as well as a set of tools, it can also be a challenge to balance between them and avoid reducing lean to the tools. "Kaizen" ("good change") is a Japanese concept used to remind people of the fact that a process or product is never perfect, never good enough. Continuous improvement is the answer. This is the same challenge as for other innovations; enjoy improvements but never stop progressing further.

Some researchers have made a distinction between "lean organizations" and "learning organizations" because the ability of an individual employee to control their own work situation is low in the former and higher in the latter, based on models from the socio-technical school (Lorentz and Lundvall 2011). However, there is also continuous learning in a lean organized model, and in the Toyota version much attention is given to ensuring a flow through the whole process. The aim of JIT is that producers will deliver what customers want when they want it, and keep storage costs low.

Lean is now adopted and used in many different settings – in both the private and public sectors, and in the US and across Europe – and interpreted by many different actors. However, the main components mentioned above are present in most versions. It still consists of continuous improvement work, in which the focus on quality and waste reduction is fundamental. Reducing time and costs are goals of this work, as they are for most of the efforts to improve efficiency in both private firms and the public sector.

Introducing lean in an organization and making it work within the everyday routines is not a quick fix; good planning is needed. Failures and unmet expectations have been reported, but proponents also report sufficient successes to keep the interest in diffusion of the principles alive. For instance, Bhatia and Drew (2006) noted that:

> In a UK government office processing large volumes of standard documents, lean techniques achieved double-digit productivity gains in the number of documents processed per hour and improved customer service by slashing lead time to fewer than 12 days, from about 40, thus eliminating backlogs. The proportion of documents processed correctly the first time increased by roughly 30 percent; lead time to process incoming mail decreased to 2 days, from 15; and the staff occasionally attains the nirvana of an unprecedented zero backlog.
>
> (p. 1)

In Aberdeenshire in Scotland, the local authority's processing of planning applications became faster and more efficient after the introduction of a "Kaizen Blitz" (Rapid Improvement Event) and adherence to lean thinking:

> The percentage of applications reaching the planner's desks in three days was increased from 2% to 100% and the productivity of the people doing the processing increased by 160%. This gave them more time to tackle the other work they never had time for before. [...]
> Another event in Social Work saved the equivalent of nine full time Social Workers across the shire by stripping out the waste associated with the generation of reports.
>
> (Improvement Service n.d., p. 3)

These two examples indicate that when lean thinking is implemented successfully, it can be a triple-win situation – for the firm or agency, for the employees and for the customers or service users. Lean fits into the principles of innovation theory in general; it is continuous, it has the focus on end-users and it tries to use the innovative capacity of employees. One criticism has been that it is incremental innovation; the focus is on improving activities we are already doing, so the continuous improvement work will not result in radical innovations. Radical decisions have to be made at the top. It can also be debated how well a production line theory from the car industry can be transferred to the service sector in which the "product" is created through interaction with service users. However, the examples above and the focus on service users seem to indicate that it is possible to overcome this challenge.

The above reports on the use of the tools employed to realize lean thinking (and the use of other simple tools and techniques as well) remind us that using tools helps us to focus on tasks close to us that can easily be organized better, and that we can sometimes be surprised by our own blindness. In both scientific management and lean, a starting point is to organize the working environment so you have what you need when you need it. That is elementary both in the car industry and in a hospital. However, the storage of the requisite materials does not always meet this requirement. For many employees in the service sector today, materials are stored electronically. We can imagine what could be saved in both time and energy if all of the required information was easily accessible, all of the software programmes were easy to understand and use, and the technology worked without breakdowns. If we compare this vision to the reality for most of us, we know where to find some time thieves, obviously guilty and with lengthy criminal records. Nevertheless, unlike the dreams in John Lennon's "Imagine", it should be possible to realize a world with fewer computer problems.

Open innovation and crowdsourcing: asking everyone

Schumpeter saw innovation as the engine in the development of capitalism, and temporary monopolies are then successes that can generate high profits. Based on this reasoning, R&D departments working in secret are important for survival in the market. Hiring the best and most creative innovators is an important strategy. For fashion firms, the best and most popular designers may be more important for sales than the CEOs.

However, large R&D departments are costly, and there will always be valuable competence outside the firm. Young people with bright new ideas are not hired in as established experts, and the development proceeds quickly. The experts of today may tomorrow be out-of-touch employees in the R&D department. The consequence of this fact is that it is better to invite the outside world in. We do not know where new ideas in the Google or Apple class will come from. "Open innovation is characterized by giving equal importance to external knowledge in comparison to internal knowledge" (Chesbrough *et al.* 2008).

A famous and much-used example is from the mining industry, in which firms had a tradition of keeping their geological data secret. A small Toronto-based mining firm, Goldcorp, was facing a problematic future and the possible closure of their gold mines. Inspired by knowledge of Linux, the worldwide operating system for computers developed as an open-source collaboration, the firm's CEO Rob McEwan arranged a competition. He put all of the secret information they had about their mines out on the internet and invited bright minds to propose where more gold could be found – enough to make the business profitable. The "Goldcorp Challenge" was launched with a total of US$375,000 in prize money available to participants who proposed the best methods and estimates. The response was remarkable. More than 1,400 competent professionals from 50 nations downloaded the data. First prize went to a partnership in Australia, far away from the Canadian mines. The contestants identified 110 target locations, half of which had not previously been identified by the company. Substantial quantities of gold were discovered in 80 per cent of them. The competition was a great success, and it transformed the underperforming mines into some of the most profitable sites in the industry (Friedman 2006; Tapscott and Williams 2010). This is used as an example of wikinomics, defined as a form of extensive collaboration and service user participation in the market (Tapscott and Williams 2010).

In this case, the best ideas were rewarded, but crowdsourcing can also be voluntary and without any reward, as was the case with the development of Linux and Wikipedia. In those instances, a large and somewhat undefined group works together on a common task. While *outsourcing* means that a hierarchical organization decides to leave some tasks to outsiders (another firm), *crowdsourcing* is based on collaborative actions between equals, and is self-organized and democratic. Access to the internet and the capacity for file-sharing are necessary conditions for crowdsourcing. Many-to-many communication is the basis; information does not pass through a central hub. Furthermore, it must be possible to codify and digitize the information, so it can then be globalized. People at the top, or in key positions, can control the information streams and reduce the discussed options in hierarchies. In an open exchange between equals, the participants can see the whole picture and propose new perspectives. If the aim is to solve a large problem through voluntary activity, it can be helpful to split the problem into smaller parts, if possible; that way, the amount of work is more manageable.

Another democratizing effect of crowdsourcing is that the ownership of what is developed and discovered is shared. In a world of patented ideas and intellectual property rights, open source and open access is making inventions available to everyone. For Linux, in the software business, this was seen as an important goal.

Crowdsourcing for new ideas has been criticized for yielding mediocre and insufficiently innovative results, as for other democratic processes (Lanier 2010). However, both Linux and the mining example above make this statement disputable, and, on the contrary, Surowiecki (2004) has argued that "under the right circumstances, groups are remarkably intelligent, and are often smarter than the smartest people in them" (p. xiii). Crowdsourcing can be used both for developing and collecting innovations, and for collecting the money to realize them. In the latter case, fundraising is also a widely used term. However, the term is also used when billionaires have parties to collect money for election campaigns in the US. Barack Obama asked for small amounts from many people, from the crowd. If we think we have a brilliant idea, we may ask for US$10 from all those people out there who agree with us. This can be a way of getting the initial investment money needed.

When we are working in a public service, we do not need to keep information secret because of the competition. However, working in social welfare and human services brings another challenge for the sharing of information; information about service users – information that can identify individuals or be damaging for groups of service users – should not be shared in public.

Nevertheless, there are still many opportunities to invite people from the outside, employees and service users to find new solutions to existing challenges. Elderly care is mentioned in Chapter 5. The demographic trend of a growing number of elderly people and a decreasing number of people to take care of them is not the main problem, seen from an innovation perspective. The problem is the perception among decision-makers that tasks have to be conducted in the same way that they have been up until now. These mentally imprisoned people need help to get out.

Open innovation should be well suited to the welfare services. It can be organized in many different ways; the NHS's use of a Change Day is just one.

Establishing and connecting networks

It is quite understandable that leaders in the public sector try to avoid risk-taking. They make no immediate profit from temporary monopolies, but they can lose money and harm service users with failures. Joining and establishing inspiration networks is a reasonable strategy for risk reduction. In these networks, they can get access to new ideas and successful projects that they can adapt in their own organizations. Success in one municipality does not guarantee success in another, but it is a good starting point. Fuglsang and Rønning (2013) distinguish between four different forms of network:

1   *Explorative networks* are where dedicated actors meet (regularly or once a year) to find inspiration and get good examples. The field of interest can cover broad topics, and the participants learn from each other.
2   *Local networks* are more oriented towards local conditions, and are based on fewer actors (such as from one municipality). The actors may know each other, both professionally and personally.
3   *Push networks* are networks within networks. They consist of smaller groups of informed and articulate actors within a given field who try to set the agenda by mobilizing actors, publishing and analysing.
4   *Social movements* are, in contrast to the other types of network, more explicit in representing particular values that they try to promote to the municipality. These groups are not "inside" the municipality; they have their support base outside, in civil society.

In theories of social networks, it is common to distinguish between weak and strong ties. Strong ties exist between family members or within groups closely connected to each other. Weak ties exist when the members are more distanced, and can be based on only one connection or "string" (such as a sporting activity or a job), whereas we have a multi-stringed connection to our relatives. Most of us need, and have, close connections to other people. However, if we only interact with people with whom we have strong ties, we will probably know what the rest of the group knows, and we get little new information through the interactions; it is a closed circle. Nevertheless, it is easy to communicate and we trust the rest of the group (Halpern 2005; Rønning and Starrin 2009). Local networks can have a closed-circle problem, while explorative networks may have less trust between the participants, though here the actors can be confronted with new information. Some people are in a strategic position, since they have the go-between function that connects different networks, and they may sometimes be the only ones. From an innovation perspective, these people are important because they can link information from two networks, bringing new information into both. They are bridging information (Halpern 2005) and can confirm "the strength of weak ties" (Granovetter 1973). Innovations can be initiated when people are challenged by new information and new possibilities.

The conclusion of this section is that participation in inspiration networks, especially when we are confronted with new ideas or ways of thinking, can stimulate innovations in our own organization.

Conclusion

In this chapter, the focus has been on the different paths to take when we want to engage in innovative work. Many paths are available, and numerous different tools and techniques can be used if we want to challenge our own way of thinking. Consultants and firms certified in using different tools and approaches earn a reasonable income through assisting organizations with innovative work. There are many such consultants and firms with high levels of competence, but we want to stress that it is better to innovate than to be innovated; we are often experts in our field, and those who best know the situation. Outsiders will more often base their approach on a general understanding of the situation. However, we may be myopic and unable to see how to change our way of working, whereas outsiders can look at our situation with a new perspective. A powerful combination can then be to try to engage insiders but ask for help from outside for specific tasks, without losing the opportunity to develop and use local competence. If we accept the need to see innovation as a way of thinking, it has to be anchored inside the organization, and inside the minds of the employees.

Technology has obviously been a driver of innovations in social welfare and human services. Human relations and communication have changed dramatically with the advent of the internet and mobile phones. This is a field in which changes are rapid. In daily work, technology is both a great help and a source of frustration. It is important for people in welfare services that if new technologies are to be implemented in a useful way, they are both incorporated into the organizational routines and seen as an improvement by employees and service users.

The organizational implementation can often need more time and work than leaders expect. It can be easily be proven that there is a gap between technological possibilities and technology's actual use in welfare services today, and this gap is probably more an organizational than an economic problem.

Heterogeneity is mentioned as a good condition for change, since different ways of thinking can challenge our established "truths". However, in a world with demands for specialized competence and a scarcity of resources, it is not easy to hire a philosopher in a medical department. To quote General Patton, "if everyone is thinking alike, then someone isn't thinking" (Patton n.d.). If that is the case, we must conclude that there may be some unused intellectual capacity in the team. Heterogeneity can be seen as a long-term investment in innovation, rather than as a short-term improvement in efficiency.

Job rotation can be a way of creating heterogeneity. People are put into jobs of which they have little or no experience. They can (or have to) ask the simple but crucial questions that insiders do not, like the boy in Hans Christian Andersen's story "The Emperor's New Clothes". The aim of job rotation is to promote rapid and efficient interactive learning and communication across functions and divisions. Job rotation can be organized within different parts of one organization, between organizations in the same field, and between different fields of operation (public–private, supplier–user, etc.) (Lundvall 2001).

There are some simple gimmicks that can give new insights into how an organization is performing. From literature, we know the trick when kings (such as in Shakespeare's *Henry V*) or other people at the top of the hierarchy disguise themselves as lay people to observe what people really think (about themselves or others). This approach is now also used as entertainment on TV (*Undercover Boss*). The same strategy, used openly, is recommended by consultants: "[T]o lead an organization that constantly strives to improve, the chief executive of a hospital, a social service agency, or a prison must therefore spend at least one day a week on the 'shop floor'" (Bhatia and Drew 2006, p. 1). A special version of this strategy is to let the boss be the patient and take him or her on the route a patient has to take from diagnosis to treatment. When hospital doctors themselves become patients, it can be a stimulant for improving the situation for patients (service users).

To create an innovative culture in an organization may take some time. However, large changes have to start somewhere, and they can start with a small change and a project that is affordable. The initial project can be used for learning, and since it is small-scale, the costs of failures are relatively easy to absorb. As an encouragement for the way ahead, we know that when we start to collect information about innovation, our organization will increase its capacity to receive more knowledge, and increase its absorptive capacity (Cohen and Levinthal 1990). And we will have started to rock the boat.

Note

1 The formulation is from Tidd *et al.* 2005.

References

Adrian, L. M. (1998). "The world we shall win for labor": early twentieth-century hobo self-publication. In Danky, J. P. and Wiegand, W. A. (eds) *Print Culture in a Diverse America*. Urbana and Chicago, IL: University of Illinois Press.

Age UK (n.d.). *Dementia and Music*. Available online at: www.ageuk.org.uk/health-wellbeing/conditions-illnesses/dementia-and-music/ (accessed 13 October 2014).

Almirall, E. and Wareham, J. (2008). Living labs and open innovation: roles and applicability. *The Electronic Journal for Virtual Organizations and Networks*, 10, 22–46.

Alvord, S. H., Brown, D. and Letts, C. W. (2004). Social entrepreneurship and societal transformation. *The Journal of Applied Behavioral Science*, 40(3), 260–282.

Amundsen, O., Aasen, T. M., Gressgård, L. J. and Hansen, K. (2011). *Medarbeiderdrevet innovasjon: en kunnskapsstatus [Employee-driven Innovation: A State-of-the-Art Report]* Report 175. Stavanger: International Research Institute of Stavanger.

Andersen, J. and Elm Larsen, J. (eds) (2004). *Socialpolitik [Social Policy]*. Copenhagen: Hans Reitzels Förlag.

Anttonen, A. (1997). The welfare state and social citizenship. In Kauppinen, T. and Gordon, T. (eds) *Unresolved Dilemmas: Women, Work and the Family in the United States, Europe and the former Soviet Union*. Aldershot: Ashgate.

Asheim, B. and Gertler, M. S. (2005). The geography of innovation: regional innovation systems. In Fagerberg, J., Movery, D. and Nelson, R. (eds) *The Oxford Handbook of Innovation*. Oxford: Oxford University Press.

Australian Public Service Commission (2007). *Tackling Wicked Problems: A Public Policy Perspective*. Canberra: Australian Public Service Commission. Available online at: www.apsc.gov.au/publications-and-media/archive/publications-archive/tackling-wicked-problems (accessed 11 October 2014).

Bamberger, P. (2008). Beyond contextualization: using context theories to narrow the micro–macro gap in management research. *Academy of Management Journal*, 51(5), 839–846.

Bason, C. (2010). *Leading Public Sector Innovation*. Bristol: The Policy Press.

Baumol, W. and Bowen, W. (1966). *Performing Arts, The Economic Dilemma: A Study of Problems Connected to Theatre, Opera, Music and Dance*. New York: Twentieth Century Fund.

Bäckstrøm, A., Davie, G., Edgardh, N. and Pettersson, P. (eds) (2011). *Welfare and Religion in 21st Century Europe: Volume 2*. Farnham: Ashgate.

Beck-Jørgensen, T. and Bozeman, B. (2007). Public value: an inventory. *Administration and Society*, 39(3), 354–381.

Becker, H. (1963). *Outsiders*. New York: The Free Press.

Behn, R. D. (2008). The adaption of innovation: the challenge of learning to adapt tacit knowledge. In Borins, S. F. (ed.) *Innovations in Government: Research, Recognition and Replication*. Washington, DC: Brookings Institution Press.

Benington, J. and Moore, M. (2011) Public value in complex and changing times. In Benington, J. and Moore, M. (eds) *Public Value: Theory and Practice*. New York: Palgrave Macmillan.

Beresford, P. (2002). User involvement in research and evaluation: liberation or regulation? *Social Policy and Society*, 1(2), 95–105.

Beresford, P. and Croft, S. (2001). Service users' knowledges and the social construction of social work. *Journal of Social Work*, 1(3), 295–316.

Bergmark, A., Bergmark, Å. and Lundstrøm, T. (2011). *Evidensbaserad socialt arbete: teori, kritikk, praktikk [Evidence-Based Social Work: Theory, Critique, Practice]*. Stockholm: Natur och Kultur.

Best, J. (2006). *Flavor of the Month: Why Smart People Fall for Fads*. Berkeley, CA: University of California Press.

Bhatia, A. and Drew, J. (2006). Applying lean production to the public sector. *The McKinsey Quarterly*. June, 1–7. Available online at: www.mckinsey.com/insights/public_sector/applying_lean_production_to_the_public_sector (accessed 13 October 2014).

Björgvinsson, E., Ehn, P. and Hillgren, P-A. (2010). *Participatory Design and "Democratizing Innovation"*. Paper presented at the Proceedings of the 11th Biennial Participatory Design Conference, Sydney, Australia.

Borglund, T., De Geer, H. and Hallvarsson, M. (2008). *Värdeskapande CSR: hur företag tar socialt ansvar [Value-Creating CSR: How Corporations Take Their Social Responsibility]*. Stockholm: Norstedts Akademiska Förlag.

Borins, S. (2001). Innovation, success and failure in public management research: some methodological reflections. *Public Management Review*, 3(1), 13–17.

Borins, S. (2008). Research on innovation in government: what next? In Borins, S. (ed.) *Innovations in Government*. Washington, DC: Brookings Institution Press.

Bornstein, D. and Davis, S. (2010). *Social Entrepreneurship: What Everyone Needs to Know*. New York: Oxford University Press.

Bovaird, T. and Löffler, E. (eds) (2003). *Public Management and Governance*. London: Routledge.

Bovaird, T. (2007). Beyond engagement and participation: user and community coproduction of public services. *Public Administration Review*, 67(5), 846–860.

Brunsson, N. (2006). *Mechanisms of Hope: Maintaining the Dream of the Rational Organization*. Malmö: Liber.

Brunsson, N. and Jacobsson, B. (1998). *Standardisering [Standardization]*. Stockholm: Nerenius and Santerus Förlag.

Burns, T. and Stalker, G. M. (1961) *The Management of Innovation*. London: Tavistock.

Busch-Geertsema, V. (2011). *Housing First Europe: Testing a Social Innovation in Tackling Homelessness in Different National and Local Contexts*. Available online at: www.housingfirst.fi/files/1276/Busch-Geertsema_2011_-_Housing_First_Europe.pdf (accessed 13 October 2014).

Busch-Geertsema, V. (2013). *Housing First Europe: Final Report*. Bremen/Brussels: GISS and The Danish National Board of Social Services.

Business Week (1998). Steve Jobs on Apple's resurgence: "not a one-man show". 12 May. Available online at: www.businessweek.com/bwdaily/dnflash/may1998/nf805 12d.htm (accessed 6 October 2014).

Campbell, D. (1979). Assessing the impact of planned social change. *Evaluation and Programme Planning*, 2(1), 67–90.

Casero-Ripollés, A. and Feenstra, R. A. (2012). The 15-M Movement and the new media: a case study of how new themes were introduced into Spanish political discourse. *MIA (Media International Australia)*, 144, 68–76. Available online at: http://repositori.uji.es/xmlui/bitstream/handle/10234/80466/53905.pdf?sequence=1 (accessed 13 October 2014).

Chan, Y. (2002). Why haven't we mastered alignment? The importance of the informal organization structures. *MIS Quarterly Executive*, 1(2), 97–112.

Charlton, B. G. (1997). Book review: *Evidence-Based Medicine: How to Practice and Teach EBM*. *Journal of Evaluation in Clinical Practice*, 3(2), 169–172.

Chesbrough, H. W. (2003). *Open Innovation: The New Imperative for Creating and Profiting from Technology*. Boston, MA: Harvard Business School Press.

Chesbrough, H., Vanhaverbeke, W. and West, J. (2008). *Open Innovation: Researching a New Paradigm*. Oxford: Oxford University Press.

Christensen, T. and Lægreid, P. (2002). Introduction: Chapter 1. In Christensen, T. and Lægreid, P. (eds) *New Public Management*. Farnham: Ashgate.

Christensen, T. and Lægreid, P. (2007). Introduction: theoretical approaches and research questions. In Christensen, T. and Lægreid, P. (eds) *Transcending New Public Management*. Burlington: Ashgate.

Cohen, M. D., March, J. G. and Olsen, J. P. (1972). A garbage can model of organizational choice. *Administrative Science Quarterly*, 17(1), 1–25.

Cohen, W. M. and Levinthal, D. A. (1990). Absorptive capacity: a new perspective on learning and innovation. *Administrative Science Quarterly*, 35(1): 128–152.

Cole, M. and Barston, G. (2006). *Unlocking Public Value*. Hoboken, NJ: John Wiley & Sons.

Conrad, P. (2007). *The Medicalization of Society*. Baltimore, MD: Johns Hopkins University Press.

Considine, M., Lewis, J. M. and Alexander, D. (2009). *Networks, Innovation and Public Policy*. Basingstoke: Palgrave Macmillan.

Cresswell, T. (2005). Moral geographies. In Atkinson, D., Jackson, P., Sibley, D. and Washbourne, N. (eds) *Cultural Geography. A Critical Dictionary of Key Concepts*. New York: I. B. Tauris.

Czarniawska, B. and Sevon, G. (1996). *Translating Organizational Change*. New York: Walter de Gruyter & Co.

Dahl Jacobsen, K. (1967). Politisk fattigdom [Political poverty]. *Kontrast*, 3(1).

Daly, M. (2011). *Welfare*. Cambridge: Polity Press.

Denvall, V., Granlöf, S., Knutagård, M., Nordfeldt, M. and Swärd, H. (2011a). Utvärdering av "Hemlöshet: många ansikten, mångas ansvar" [Evaluation of "Homelessness: Many Faces, the Responsibility of Many"]. Final report. Lund: Socialhögskolan. Available online at: www.soch.lu.se/images/Socialhogskolan/MS2011_2.pdf (accessed 13 October 2014).

Denvall, V., Heule, C. and Kristiansen, A. (2007). Brukaren och socialarbetarutbildningen [The user and the education of social workers]. In Svensson, K. (ed.) *Normer och normalitet i socialt arbete* [*Norms and Normality in Social Work*]. Lund: Studentlitteratur.

Denvall, V., Heule, C. and Kristiansen, A. (2011b). Mobilisering inom socialarbetarutbildningen [Mobilization of social work education]. In Denvall, V., Heule, C. and Kristiansen, A. (eds) *Social mobilisering: en utmaning för socialt arbete* [*Social Mobilization: A Challenge for Social Work*]. Malmö: Gleerups Utbildning.

Digmann, A. (2010). *Danmarks mest innovative kommune* [*The Most Innovative Municipality in Denmark*]. Conference paper, conference organized by the Danish Leadership Academy, 6–7 December.

Drejer, I. (2004). Identifying innovation in surveys of services: a Schumpeterian perspective. *Research Policy*, 33(3), 551–562.

Dreyfus, H. and Dreyfus, S. (1986). *Mind over Machine*. New York: The Free Press.

Driver, F. (1988). Moral geographies: social science and the urban environment in mid-nineteenth century England. *Transactions of the Institute of British Geographers*, 13(3), 275–287.

Drucker, P. (1954). *The Practice of Management*. New York: Harper Business.

EACEA (2013). Leonardo da Vinci Multilateral Projects for Development of Innovation. Available online at: http://eacea.ec.europa.eu/llp/leonardo/leonardo_da_vinci_multilateral_projects_en.php (accessed 13 October 2014).

Earl, L. (2002). *Innovation and Change in the Public Sector: A Seeming Oxymoron: Survey of Electronic Commerce and Technology*. Ottawa: Statistics Canada.

Earl, L. (2004). *A Historical Comparison of Technological Change, 1998–2000 and 2000–2002, in the Private and Public Sectors*. Ottawa: Statistics Canada.

Easton, D. (1953). *The Political System*. New York: Knopf.

Echeverri, P. and Skålen, P. (2011). Co-creation and co-destruction: a practice-theory based study of interactive value formation. *Marketing Theory*, 11(3), 351–373.

Edelman, M. (1985). *The Symbolic Uses of Politics*. Urbana and Chicago, IL: University of Illinois Press.

Ekvall, G. (1996). Organizational climate for creativity and innovation. *European Journal of Work and Organizational Psychology*, 5(1), 105–123.

Eriksson-Zetterquist, U. (2009). *Institutionell teori: idéer, moden, förändring* [*Institutional Theory: Ideas, Fashion, Change*]. Malmö: Liber.

Esping-Andersen, G. (1990). *The Three Worlds of Welfare Capitalism*. Cambridge: Polity Press.

Ettlie, J. E., Bridges, W. P. and O'Keefe, R. D. (1984). Organization strategy and structural differences for radical versus incremental innovation. *Management Science*, 30(6), 682–695.

European Commission (EC) (2010). European Platform against Poverty and Social Exclusion. Available online at: http://ec.europa.eu/social/main.jsp?catId=961 (accessed 11 October 2014).

Evers, A., Ewert, B. and Brandsen, T. (eds) (2014). *Social Innovations for Social Cohesion: Transnational Patterns and Approaches from 20 European Cities*. Available online at: www.wilcoproject.eu/downloads/WILCO-project-eReader.pdf (accessed 11 October 2014).

Fagerberg, J. and Verspagen, B. (2009). Innovation studies: the emerging structure of a new scientific field. *Research Policy*, 38(2), 218–233.

Florida, R. L. (2002). *The Rise of the Creative Class*. New York: Basic Books.

Florida, R. L. (2008). *Who's Your City: How the Creative Economy Is Making Where to Live the Most Important Decision of Your Life*. New York: Basic Books.

France Info (2004). 16 April.

Franz, H-W., Hochgerner, J. and Howaldt, J. (2012). Challenging social innovation: an introduction. In Franz, H-W., Hochgerner, J. and Howaldt, J. (eds) *Challenging Social Innovation: Potentials for Business, Social Entrepreneurship, Welfare and Civil Society*. Berlin: Springer.

Friedland, R. and Boden, D. (1994). NowHere: an introduction to space, time and modernity. In Friedland, R. and Boden, D. (eds) *NowHere: Space, Time and Modernity*. Berkeley, CA: University of California Press.

Friedman, T. L. (2006). *The World is Flat: A Brief History of the Twenty-First Century*, updated and expanded edition. New York: Farrar, Strauss & Giroux.

Fuglsang, L. (2010). Bricolage and invisible innovation in public service innovation. *Journal of Innovation Economics*, 5, 67–87. Available online at: www.cairn.info/revue-journal-of-innovation-economics-2010-1-page-67.htm (accessed 13 October 2013).

Fuglsang, L. and Rønning, R. (2013). Inspirasjonsnettverk og reduksjon av usikkerhet [Inspiration networks and the reduction of uncertainty]. In Ringholm, T., Teigen, H. and Aarsæther, N. (eds) *Innovative kommuner [Innovative Municipalities]*. Oslo: Cappelen/Damm Akademisk.

Fuglsang, L. and Rønning, R. (2014). Conclusion: public sector service innovation in context. In Fuglsang, L., Rønning, R. and Enquist, B. (eds) *Framing Innovation in Public Service Sectors*. New York: Routledge.

Gallouj, F. and Toivonen, M. (2011). Elaborating the characteristics-based approach to service innovation: making the service process visible. *Journal of Innovation Economics*, 8(2), 33–58. Available online at: www.cairn.info/revue-journal-of-innovation-economics-2011-2-page-33.htm (accessed 11 October 2014).

Gibbons, M., Limoges, C., Novotny, H., Schartzman, S., Scott, P. and Trow, M. (1994). *The New Production of Knowledge: The Dynamics of Science and Research in Contemporary Societies*. London: SAGE.

Gidron, B. and Hasenfeld, Y. (2012). Managing conflicting institutional logics: social service versus market. In Gidron, B. and Hasenfeld, Y. (eds) *Social Enterprises: An Organizational Perspective*. Basingstoke: Palgrave Macmillan.

Gore, A. (2007). Speech after receiving the Nobel Peace Prize in Oslo. Available online at: www.nobelprize.org/nobel_prizes/peace/laureates/2007/gore-lecture_en.html (accessed 13 October 2014).

Granovetter, M. (1973). The strength of weak ties. *American Journal of Sociology*, 78(6), 1360–1380.

Gray, M., Plath, D. and Webb, S. A. (2009). *Evidence Based Social Work: A Critical Stance*. London: Routledge.

Greenwood, R., Oliver, C., Sahlin, K. and Suddaby, R. (2008). Introduction. In Greenwood, R. (ed.) *The SAGE Handbook of Organizational Institutionalism*. London: SAGE.

Habermas, J. (1991). *The Structural Transformation of the Public Sphere*. Boston, MA: The MIT Press.

Hagen, A. L. (2014). *Fear and Magic in Architects' Utopia: The Power of Creativity among Snøhettas of Oslo and New York*. PhD thesis, University of Oslo.

Halpern, D. (2005). *Social Capital*. Bristol: Polity Press.

Halpin, J. F. (1966). *Zero Defects: A New Dimension in Quality Assurance*. New York: McGraw-Hill.

Halvorsen, T., Hauknes, J., Miles, I. and Røste, R. (2005). *On the Difference between Public and Private Sector Innovation*. Public Report No. D9. Oslo: NIFU STEP.

Hanks, S. and Swithinbank, T. (1997). *The Big Issue* and other street papers: a response to homelessness. *Environment and Urbanization*, 9(1), 149–158.

Hardy, C. and Maguire, S. (2008). Institutional entrepreneurship. In Greenwood, R. (ed.) *The SAGE Handbook of Organizational Institutionalism*. London: SAGE.

Harris, K. (1995). *Collected Quotes from Albert Einstein*. Available online at: http://rescomp.stanford.edu/~cheshire/EinsteinQuotes.html (accessed 7 October 2014).

Hartley, J. (2005). Innovation in governance and public services: past and present. *Public Money and Management*, 25(1), 27–34.

Hartley, J. (2008). The innovation landscape for public service organizations. In Hartley, J., Donaldson, C., Skelcher, C. and Wallace, M. (eds) *Managing to Improve Public Services*. Cambridge: Cambridge University Press.

Hartley, J., Donaldson, C., Skelcher, C. and Wallace, M. (2008). *Managing to Improve Public Services*. Cambridge: Cambridge University Press.

Hauser, G. (1998). Vernacular dialogue and the rhetoric of public opinion. *Communication Monographs*, 65(3), 87–107.

Heinz, T. L. (2004). Street newspapers. In Levinson, D. (ed.) *Encyclopaedia of Homelessness*. London: SAGE.

Helpman, E. (2004). *The Mystery of Economic Growth*. Cambridge, MA: Harvard University Press.

Heule, C., Knutagård, M. and Kristiansen, A. (forthcoming). Gap-mending pedagogy in social work education.

Hill, T. P. (1977). On goods and services. *Review of Income and Wealth*, 23(4), 315–338.

Hood, C. (1991). A public management for all seasons? *Public Administration*, 69(1), 3–19.

Howley, K. (2003). A poverty of voices: street papers as communicative democracy. *Journalism*, 4(3), 273–292.

Hubert, A. (2010). *Empowering People, Driving Change: Social Innovation in the European Union*. Luxembourg: Bureau of European Policy Advisers.

Hulgård, L. and Shajahan, P. K. (2013). Social innovation for people-centred development. In Moulaert, F., MacCallum, D., Mehmood, A. and Hamdouch, A. (eds) *The International Handbook on Social Innovation: Collective Action, Social Learning and Transdisciplinary Research*. Cheltenham: Edward Elgar.

Høyrup, S. (2012). Employee-driven innovation: a new phenomenon, concept and mode of innovation. In Høyrup, S., Bonnafous-Boucher, M., Hasse, C., Lotz, M. and Møller, K. (eds) *Employee-Driven Innovation: A New Approach*. Basingstoke: Palgrave Macmillan.

Improvement Service (n.d.). *Lean Thinking and Practice in a Scottish Local Authority*. Available online at: www.improvementservice.org.uk/library/download-document/2265-case-study-lean-thinking-and-practice-in-a-scottish-local-authority/ (accessed 8 October 2014).

Jay, A. (2012). *Oxford Dictionary of Political Quotations*. Oxford: Oxford University Press.

Jensen, K. E., Jensen, J. P., Digman, A. and Bendix, H. W. (2008). *Prinsipper for offentlig innovation* [*Principles for Public Innovation*]. Copenhagen: Børsens Förlag.

Jessop, B., Moulaert, F., Hulgård, L. and Hamdouch, A. (2013). Social innovation research: a new stage in innovation analysis? In Moulaert, F., MacCallum, D., Mehmood, A. and Hamdouch, A. (eds) *The International Handbook on Social Innovation: Collective Action, Social Learning and Transdisciplinary Research*. Cheltenham: Edward Elgar.

Jiang, P., Chen, Y., Xu, B., Dong, W. and Kennedy, E. (2013). Building low carbon communities in China: the role of individual's behaviour change and engagement. *Energy Policy*, 60, 611–620.

Johansson, H. (2008). *Socialpolitikens klassiker* [*The Classics in Social Policy*]. Stockholm: Liber.

Johnsson, B. (2010). *Kampen om sjukfrånvaron* [*The Fight against Sickness Absence*]. Lund: Arkiv Förlag.

Juul Kristensen, C. and Voxted, S. (2009). *Innovation: medarbejder og burger* [*Innovation: Employee and User*]. Copenhagen: Hans Reitzel.

Jönsson, L-E., Persson, A. and Sahlin, K. (2011). *Institution*. Malmö: Liber.

Karlsson, M. (2006). *Självhjälpsgrupper* [*Self-Help Groups*]. Lund: Studentlitteratur.

Kingdom, J. (1999). *Government and Politics in Britain: An Introduction*. Cambridge: Polity Press.

Kingdon, J. W. (2003). *Agendas, Alternatives and Public Policies*, second edition. New York: Longman.

Klausen, K. K. (2001). New Public Management: en fortolkningsramme for reformer. [New Public Management: a framework for understanding reforms]. In Busch, T. (ed.) *Modernisering av offentlig sector: New Public Management i praksis* [*Modernization of the Public Sector: New Public Management in Practice*]. Oslo: Universitetsforlaget.

Klein, J-L. (2013). Introduction: social innovation at the crossroads between science, economy and society. In Moulaert, F., MacCallum, D., Mehmood, A. and Hamdouch, A. (eds) *The International Handbook on Social Innovation: Collective Action, Social Learning and Transdisciplinary Research*. Cheltenham: Edward Elgar.

Knutagård, M. (2009). *Skälens fångar: hemlöshetsarbetets organisering, kategoriseringar och förklaringar* [*Prisoners of Reason: Organization, Categorizations and Explanations of Work with the Homeless*]. Malmö: Égalité.

Knutagård, M. (2013). Det sociala arbetets moraliska geografi [The moral geography of social work]. In Linde, S. and Svensson, K. (eds) *Förändringens entreprenörer och tröghetens agenter: människobehandlande organisationer ur ett nyinstitutionellt perspektiv* [*Entrepreneurs of Change and Agents of Inertia: Human Service Organizations from a Institutional Perspective*]. Stockholm: Liber.

Knutagård, M. and Kristiansen, A. (2013). Not by the book: the emergence and translation of Housing First in Sweden. *European Journal of Homelessness*, 7(1), 93–115.

Koch, P., Cunningham, P., Schwabsky, N. and Hauknes, J. (2005) *Innovation in the Public Sector: Summary and Policy Recommendations*. Public Report No. D24. Oslo: NIFU STEP.

Kooiman, J. (2003). *Governing as Governance*. London: SAGE.

Krafcik, J. (1988). Triumph of the lean production system. *Sloan Management Review*, 30(1), 41–52.

Kramer, R. M. and Cook, K. S. (eds) (2004). *Trust and Distrust in Organizations: Dilemmas and Approaches*. New York: Russell Sage Foundation.

Kuhn, R. and Culhane, D. P. (1998). Applying cluster analysis to test a typology of homelessness by pattern of shelter utilization: results from the analysis of administrative data. *American Journal of Community Psychology*, 26(2), 207–232.

Kuhn, T. S. (1962). *Structure of Scientific Revolutions*. Chicago, IL: University of Chicago Press.

Lanier, J. (2010). *You Are Not a Gadget*. New York: Penguin.

Levitan, S. A. and Johnson, C. M. (1984). *Beyond the Safety Net: Reviving the Promise of Opportunity in America*. Cambridge, MA: Ballinger.

Lindblom, C. E. (1979). Still muddling, not yet through. *Public Administration Review*, 39(6), 517–526.

Lindemann, K. (2007). A tough sell: stigma as souvenir in the contested performances of San Francisco's homeless street sheet vendors. *Text and Performance Quarterly*, 27(1), 41–57.

Lipsky, M. (1980). *Street Level Bureaucracy*. New York: Russell Sage Foundation.

Lorentz, E. and Lundvall, B-Å. (2011). Accounting for creativity in the European Union: a multilevel analysis of individual competence, labour market structures and systems of education and training. *Cambridge Journal of Economics*, 35(2), 269–297.

Lukes, S. (2005). *Power: A Radical View*. Basingstoke: Palgrave Macmillan.

Lundvall, B-Å. (1988). Innovation as an interactive process: from user–producer interaction to national system of innovation. In Dosi, G., Freeman, C., Nelson, R., Silverberg, G. and Soete, L. (eds) *Technical Change and Economic Theory*. London: Pinter Publishers.

Lundvall, B-Å. (2001). *Job Rotation in the Learning Economy*. Presentation in Brussels, September.

Lundvall, B-Å. (2013). Evolution, developments and key issues. In Fagerberg, J., Martin, B. and Sloth Andersen, E. (eds) *Innovation Studies: Evolution & Future Challenges.* Oxford: Oxford University Press.

Magnusson, J. (2002). *Ny situation – ny organisation: gatutidningen Situation Sthlm 1995–2000 [New Situation – New Organization: The Street Paper Situation Stockholm 1995–2000]*. PhD thesis, Lund University.

Majone, G. (1994). The rise of the regulatory state in Europe. *West European Politics*, 17(3), 77–101.

Martin, R. L. and Osberg, S. (2007). Social entrepreneurship: the case for definition. *Stanford Social Innovation Review*, 5(2), 28–39.

Martinelli, F. (2012). Social innovation or social exclusion? Innovating social services in the context of a retrenching welfare state. In Franz, H-W., Hochgerner, J. and Howaldt, J. (eds) *Challenge Social Innovation: Potentials for Business, Social Entrepreneurship, Welfare and Civil Society*. Berlin and Heidelberg: Springer Berlin Heidelberg.

Mayes, R. and Horwitz, A. (2005). DSM-III and the revolution in the classification of mental illness. *Journal of the History of the Behavioral Sciences*, 41(3), 249–268.

Mazzucato, M. (2013). *The Entrepreneurial State: Debunking Public vs. Private Sector Myths*. London: Anthem Press.

Meeuwisse, A. (1997). *Vänskap och organisering: en studie av Fountain Houserörelsen [Friendship and Organization: A Study of the Fountain House Movement]*. Lund: Arkiv Förlag.

Meeuwisse, A. and Sunesson, S. (1998). Frivilliga organisationer, socialt arbete och expertis [Voluntary organizations, social work and expertise]. *Socialvetenskaplig Tidskrift [Social Sciences Journal]*, 2–3, 172–193.

Mik-Meyer, N. and Villadsen, K. (2013). *Power and Welfare: Understanding Citizens' Encounters with State Welfare*. London: Routledge.

Misztal, B. A. (1996). *Trust in Modern Societies: The Search for the Bases of Social Order*. Oxford: Polity Press.

Moilanen, T. and Salminen, A. (2007). *Comparative Study on the Public Service Ethics of the EU Member States*. Research and Studies 1. Helsinki: Ministry of Finance.

Monbiot, G. (2000). *Captive State*. London: Macmillan.

Moore Jr, B. (1984). *Privacy: Studies in Social and Cultural History*. New York: M.E. Sharpe.

Moore, M. (1995). *Creating Public Value: Strategic Management in Government*. Cambridge, MA: Harvard University Press.

Moore, M. and Hartley, J. (2011). Innovations in governance. In Osborne, S. (ed.) *The New Public Governance?* London: Routledge.

Moulaert, F., MacCallum, D. and Hillier, J. (2013). Social innovation: intuition, precept, concept, theory and practice. In Moulaert, F., MacCallum, D., Mehmood, A. and Hamdouch, A. (eds) *The International Handbook on Social Innovation: Collective Action, Social Learning and Transdisciplinary Research.* Cheltenham: Edward Elgar.

Moulaert, F., Martinelli, F., Swyngedouw, E. and Gonzalez, S. (2005). Towards alternative model(s) of local innovation. *Urban Studies,* 42(11), 1969–1990.

Mulgan, G. (2006). The process of social innovation. *Innovations: Technology, Governance, Globalization,* 1(2), 145–162.

Mulgan, G. (2012). Social innovation theories: can theory catch up with practice? In Franz, H-W., Hochgerner, J. and Howaldt, J. (eds) *Challenge Social Innovation: Potentials for Business, Social Entrepreneurship, Welfare and Civil Society.* Berlin and Heidelberg: Springer Berlin Heidelberg.

Mumford, M. D. (2002). Social innovation: ten cases from Benjamin Franklin. *Creativity Research Journal,* 14(2), 253–266.

Mumford, M. D. and Moertl, P. (2003). Cases of social innovation: lessons from two innovations in the 20th century. *Creativity Research Journal,* 15(2–3), 261–266.

Murray, R., Caulier-Grice, J. and Mulgan, G. (2010). *The Open Book of Social Innovation.* The Young Foundations & NESTA. Available online at: www.nesta.org.uk/library/documents/Social_Innovator_020310.pdf (accessed 12 October 2014).

Nelson, R. R. (2011). The moon and the ghetto revisited. *Science and Public Policy,* 38(9), 681–690.

Noddings, N. (1984). *Caring.* Berkeley, CA: University of California Press.

Nordstrøm, K. and Ridderstråle, J. (1999). *Funky Business.* Stockholm: Bookhouse Publishing.

NOU 2011:11 (2011). *Innovasjon i omsorg [Innovation in Caring].* Green Paper to the Norwegian Government.

Nozick, R. (1974). *Anarchy, State and Utopia.* New York: Basic Books.

Nygård, M. (2013). *Socialpolitik i Norden: en introduktion [Social Policy in the Nordic Countries: An Introduction].* Lund: Studentlitteratur.

Olofsson, J. (2009). *Socialpolitik: varför, hur och till vilken nytta? [Social Policy: Why, How and of What Use?].* Stockholm: SNS Förlag.

Osborne, D. and Gaebler, T. (1993). *Reinventing Government: How the Entrepreneurial Spirit is Transforming the Public Sector.* New York: Plume Books.

Osborne, S. (2010). Introduction: the (new) public governance – a suitable case for treatment? In Osborne, S. (ed.) *The New Public Governance?* London: Routledge.

Palast, G. (2002). *The Best Democracy Money Can Buy.* London: Pluto Press.

Parlette, V. (2010). *Toronto Street News* as a counterpublic sphere. In Howley, K. (ed.) *Understanding Community Media.* London: SAGE.

Patton Jr, G. S. (n.d.). *General George S. Patton Jr Quotations.* Available online at: www.generalpatton.com/quotes (accessed 13 October 2014).

Peters, G. (2010). Meta-governance and public management. In Osborne, S. (ed.) *The New Public Governance?* London: Routledge.

Philip, N. H. M. and Hussain, M. (2011). The role of digital media. *Journal of Democracy,* 22(3), 35–48.

Phills, J. A., Deiglmeier, K. and Miller, D. T. (2008). Rediscovering social innovation. *Stanford Social Innovation Review,* 6(4), 34–43.

Philo, C. (1986). *"The Same and the Other": On Geographies, Madness and Outsiders.* Occasional Paper 11. Loughborough University of Technology, Department of Geography, University of Cambridge.

Pierson, P. (2004). *Politics in Time: History, Institutions and Social Analysis*. Princeton, NJ: Princeton University Press.

Pierson, C. and Castles, F. G. (eds) (2006). *The Welfare State Reader*, second edition. Cambridge: Polity Press.

Pleace, N. (2012). *Housing First: European Observatory on Homelessness*. New York: Rosenfeld Media.

Polaine, A., Løvlie, I. and Reason, B. (2013). *Service Design: From Insights to Implementation*. New York: Rosenfeld Media.

Pollitt, C. and Bouckhaert, G. (2000). *Public Management Reform*. Oxford: Oxford University Press.

Popper, K. (1945). *The Open Society and Its Enemies*. London: Routledge.

Quist, J. (2014). *Onödig efterfrågan innom Försäkringskassan och Skatteverket* [*Unnecessary Demands within the Social Security and Tax Authorities*]. Report No. 14. Stockholm: Inspektionen fö Socialförsäkringen.

Rawls, J. (1971). *A Theory of Justice*. Oxford: Oxford University Press.

Richardson, E. A., Pearce, J., Mitchell, R. and Shortt, N. K. (2013). A regional measure of neighborhood multiple environmental deprivation: relationships with health and health inequalities. *The Professional Geographer*, 65(1), 153–170.

Ridderstråle, J. and Nordstrøm, K. (2004). *Karaoke Capitalism*. Stockholm: Bookhouse Publishing Ltd.

Ridderstråle, J. and Nordström, K. (2008). *Funky Business Forever: How to Enjoy Capitalism*, third edition. Harlow: Financial Times/Prentice-Hall.

Ritzer, G. (1998). *The McDonaldization Thesis*. Thousand Oaks, CA: SAGE.

Rizvi, G. (2008). Innovation in government: serving citizens and strengthening democracy. In Borins, S. (ed.) *Innovations in Government: Research, Recognition and Replication*. Washington, DC: Brookings Institution Press.

Rogers, E. (2003). *Diffusion of Innovations*. New York: The Free Press.

Rothwell, R., Freeman, C., Horlsey, A., Jervis, V. T. P., Robertson, A. B. and Townsend, J. (1974). SAPPHO updated: project SAPPHO phase II. *Research Policy*, 3(3), 258–291.

Rousseau, J-J. (1972). *Du contrat social* [*Of the Social Contract*]. Oxford: Clarendon Press.

Rubalcaba, L. (2007). *The New Service Economy*. Cheltenham: Edward Elgar.

Rubalcaba, L. and Di Meglio, G. (2009). Service in EU competition policy. *Journal of Service Sciences*, 1(2), 121–146.

Røhnebæk, M. (2014). *Standardized Flexibility*. PhD thesis, University of Oslo.

Rønning, R. (2009). Framtidas omsorg: noen scenarier [Care in the future: some scenarios]. *Aldring og livsløp*, 2, 2–8.

Rønning, R. (2014). The diffusion of innovation: a question of power. In Fuglsang, L., Rønning, R. and Enquist, B. (eds) *Framing Innovations in Public Service Sectors*. New York: Routledge.

Rønning, R. and Solheim, L. J. (1998). *Hjelp på egne premissser? Om brukermedvirning i velferdssektoren* [*Help on Their Own Terms? On User Involvement in the Welfare Services*]. Oslo: Universitetsforlaget.

Rønning, R. and Starrin, B. (2009). Sosial capital: et nyttig begrep [Social capital: a useful concept]. In Rønning, R. and Starrin, B. (eds) *Sosial kapital i et velferdsperspektiv* [*Social Capital in a Welfare Perspective*]. Oslo: Gyldendal Akademisk.

Sahlin, I. (1996). *På gränsen till bostad: avvisning, utvisning, specialkontrakt* [*On the Border of Housing: Rejection, Eviction, Special Contract*]. PhD thesis. Lund: Arkiv Förlag.

Salonen, T. (1998). Klient [Client]. In Denvall, V. and Jacobson, T. (eds) *Vardagsbegrepp i socialt arbete: ideologi, teori och praktik* [*Everyday Concepts in Social Work: Ideology, Theory and Practice*]. Stockholm: Norstedts Juridik.

Schaffer, B. B. and Huang, W. (1975). Distribution and the theory of access. *Development and Change*, 6(2), 13–36.

Schumpeter, J. (1934). *The Theory of Economic Development*. Cambridge, MA: Harvard University Press.

Schumpeter, J. (1943). *Capitalism, Socialism and Democracy*. New York: Harper Torchbooks.

Science Communication Unit, University of the West of England, Bristol (2014). *Science for Environment Policy In-Depth Report: Social Innovation and the Environment*. Report produced for the European Commission DG Environment, February 2014. Available online at: http://ec.europa.eu/science-environment-policy (accessed 12 October 2014).

Selznick, P. (1949). *TVA and the Grassroots*. Berkeley, CA: University of California Press.

Senge, P. M. (1990). *The Fifth Discipline: The Art and Practice of the Learning Organization*. New York: Doubleday/Currency.

Sewell, W. H. (1996). Three temporalities: toward an eventful society. In McDonald, T. (ed.) *The Historic Turn in the Human Sciences*. Ann Arbor, MI: University of Michigan Press.

Soete, L. (2013). Is innovation always good? In Fagerberg, J., Martin, B. and Sloth Andersen, E. (eds) *Innovation Studies: Evolution & Future Challenges*. Oxford: Oxford University Press.

SOU 2009:89 (2009). *Gränslandet mellan sjukdom och arbete* [*The Border between Sickness and Work*]. Green Paper to the Swedish Government.

Stanhope, V. and Dunn, K. (2011). The curious case of Housing First: the limits of evidence based policy. *International Journal of Law and Psychiatry*, 34(4), 275–282.

Sundbo, J. (2002). The service economy. *The Service Industries Journal*, 29(4), 93–116.

Sundbo, J. (2008). Innovation and involvement in service. In Fuglsang, L. (ed.) *Innovation and the Creative Process*. Cheltenham: Edward Elgar.

Surowiecki, J. (2004). *The Wisdom of the Crowds*. London: Abacus.

Svensson, P. and Bengtsson, L. (2010). Users' influence in social service innovations: two Swedish case studies. *Journal of Social Entrepreneurship*, 1(2), 190–212.

Swithinbank, T. (2001). *Coming up from the Streets: The Story of The Big Issue*. London: Earthscan.

Swärd, H. (2004). När de utsatta får en röst i medier: den nordiska gatutidningsrörelsen [The Nordic street paper movement: when the vulnerable get a voice in the media]. In Blomberg, H., Kroll, C., Lundström, T. and Swärd, H. (eds) *Sociala problem och socialpolitik i massmedier* [*Social Problems and Social Policy in the Mass Media*]. Lund: Studentlitteratur.

Sydney Morning Herald (2005). Editorial. 22 October.

Takeuchi, H. and Nonaka, I. (1986). The new new product development game. *Harvard Business Review*, January–February, 137–146.

Tapscott, D. and Williams, A. D. (2008). *Wikinomics: How Mass Communication Changes Everything*. New York: Penguin.

Taylor, J. B. (1970). Introducing social innovation. *Journal of Applied Behavioral Science*, 6(1), 69–77.

Thörn, C. (2011). Soft policies of exclusion: entrepreneurial strategies of ambience and control of public space in Gothenburg, Sweden. *Urban Geography*, 32(7), 989–1008.

Tidd, J., Bessant, J. and Pavitt, K. (2005). *Managing Innovation*. Chichester: John Wiley & Sons.

Timmermans, S. and Berg, M. (2003). *The Gold Standard*. Philadelphia, PA: Temple University Press.

Toivonen, M., Toiminen, T. and Brax, S. (2007). Innovation process interlinked with the process of service delivery: a management challenge in KIBS. *Economies and Societies*, 8(3), 355–384.

Torck, D. (2001). Voices of homeless people in street newspapers: a cross-cultural exploration. *Discourse & Society*, 12(3), 371–392.

Tsemberis, S. J. (2010). *Housing First: The Pathways Model to End Homelessness for People with Mental Illness and Addiction*. Center City, MN: Hazelden.

Ulfvarsson, J. (2004). *Drug Treatment of the Elderly: The Need for Changing Behaviour among Providers and Patients*. PhD thesis. Stockholm: Karolinska Institutet. Available online at: http://diss.kib.ki.se/2004/91-7140-010-9/ (accessed 13 October 2014).

Van Wart, M. (1996). "Reinventing" the public sector: the critical role of value restructuring. *Public Administration Quarterly*, 19(4), 456–478.

Vargo, S. L. and Lusch, R. F. (2004). Evolving to a new dominant logic for marketing. *Journal of Marketing*, 68(1), 1–17.

Varney, D. and van Vliet, W. (2008). Homelessness, children, and youth: research in the United States and Canada. *American Behavioral Scientist*, 51(6), 715–720.

Veggeland, N. (2009). *Taming the Regulatory State: Politics and Ethics*. Cheltenham: Edward Elgar.

Vitale, T. and Membretti, A. (2013). Just another roll of the dice: a socially creative initiative to assure Roma housing in North Western Italy. In Moulaert, F., MacCallum, D., Mehmood, A. and Hamdouch, A. (eds) *The International Handbook on Social Innovation: Collective Action, Social Learning and Transdisciplinary Research*. Cheltenham: Edward Elgar.

von Hippel, E. (1994). "Sticky information" and the locus of problem solving: implications for innovation. *Management Science*, 40(4), 429–439.

von Hippel, E. (2005). Democratizing innovation: the evolving phenomenon of user innovation. *Journal für Betriebswirtschaft* [*Journal of Business Management*], 55(1), 63–78.

von Hippel, E., Ogawa, S. and de Jong, J. P. J. (2011). The age of the consumer-innovator. *MIT Sloan Management Review*, 53(1), 27–35.

Weber, M. (1964). *The Theory of Social and Economic Organization*. New York: The Free Press.

Wetter-Edman, K. (2014). *Design for Service: A Framework for Articulating Designers' Contributions as Interpreters of Users' Experience*. PhD thesis, University of Gothenburg.

Wijkström, F. and Einarsson, T. (2006). *Från nationalstat till näringsliv: det civila samhällets organisationsliv i förändring* [*From National State to Business: Organizational Activity in Civil Society in Transition*]. Stockholm: Ekonomiska Forskningsinstitutet (EFI), Handelshögskolan i Stockholm.

Windrum, P. (2008). Innovation and entrepreneurship in public services. In Windrum, P. and Koch, P. M. (eds) *Innovation in Public Sector Services: Entrepreneurship, Creativity and Management*. Cheltenham: Edward Elgar.

Wodiczko, K. (1999). *Critical Vehicles: Writings, Projects, Interviews*. Boston, MA: The MIT Press.

Womack, J. P. and Jones, T. J. (2003). *Lean Thinking: Banish Waste and Create Wealth in Your Corporation.* New York: The Free Press.

Yunus, M. (2010). *Building Social Business: The New Kind of Capitalism that Serves Humanity's Most Pressing Needs.* Dhaka: Dhaka University Press.

Zahra, S. A., Gedajlovic, E., Neubaum, D. O. and Shulman, J. M. (2009). A typology of social entrepreneurs: motives, search processes and ethical challenges. *Journal of Business Venturing*, 24(5), 519–532.

Zealand Care (2014). 27 March. Available online at: www.zealandcare.dk (accessed 27 March 2014).

Zola, I. K. (1972). Medicine as an institution of social control. *Sociological Review*, 20(4), 487–504.

Websites

https://changeday.nhs.uk/healthcareradicals
http://christian-quotes.ochristian.com/Catherine-Booth-Quotes/
www.icehotel.com
www.powerus.se
www.rebelsatwork.com
www.socialinnovationeurope.eu

Index

Page numbers in **bold** denote figures.

For Product Safety Concerns and Information please contact our EU
representative GPSR@taylorandfrancis.com
Taylor & Francis Verlag GmbH, Kaufingerstraße 24, 80331 München, Germany